Tradition » Passion » Perfection

Giles Fallowfield is an acknowledged expert on champagne. He has been the consultant on Champagne for Oz Clarke's *Pocket Wine Book* since the 2001 edition and is a regular contributor to *Imbibe* and *Square Meal Magazine*, overseeing their annual champagne supplements. His work also appears in *Drinks International, Decanter, The Drinks Business, Harpers, The Times* and *The Daily Telegraph*. He won the Lanson 'Champagne Writer of the Year Award' in 2001 and 2003. His website is www.champagneguru.co.uk

Conceived and produced by
Elwin Street Productions
144 Liverpool Road
London N1 1LA
www.elwinstreet.com

Hardie Grant Books (Australia)
658 Church St
Richmond
Victoria 3121
www.hardiegrant.com.au

Hardie Grant Books (UK)
34–35 Southhampton Street
London WC2E 7HF
www.hardiegrant.co.uk

ISBN: 978-174270170-7

Series styling and art direction: Simon Daley
Illustrations: Tonwen Jones

Picture credits:
Champagne Marguet Père & Fils: p. 115; Collection CIVC:
p. 18 (Michel Guillard), 76 (Visuel Impact), 90 (Michel
Guillard); Photolibrary.com: p. 44

Recipes supplied by:
St Pancras Grand Champagne Bar (Blushing Bubbles and
French 75) and Texture Bar (Luxury Mojito and
Champolitain)

Printed in China

CHAMPAGNE

Giles Fallowfield

hardie grant books

MELBOURNE · LONDON

Contents

Why be a snob about champagne?

Champagne is one of the world's great white wines. It enjoys a unique position as 'the' drink of celebration, but today is also increasingly seen as a fine wine with a myriad of different styles. Knowing more about the wines and styles that are available will enhance your appreciation, expand the occasions on which you drink it and increase your enjoyment when you do.

At its glorious best champagne – particularly vintage champagne near the peak of its maturity, as some of the best 1988s currently are – can provide a drinking experience without equal. That magical combination of initial freshness with the Burgundy-like wine complexities champagne tends to develop with age.

Although high-quality sparkling wine is made in quite a few different countries, it is widely accepted that the world's most celebrated and sought-after examples all come from within the Champagne appellation in north-east France. Nowhere else regularly turns out sparkling wines of such intensity and complexity, that are also long lasting, thanks partly to their high natural acidity.

What is it that makes champagne special and helps to distinguish it from other quality sparkling wines? A simple answer is 'cool climate', which lies at the heart of champagne production and in part explains how it originally came to be made. In the early days of winemaking in this cool northerly region, the first alcoholic fermentation would grind to a halt as the temperature dropped with the onset of winter, often before it was complete and the natural yeasts had turned all the sugar in the grapes into alcohol. When spring arrived and the temperatures started to rise, the wines, already in bottle, would start to ferment again, giving them a slight spritz.

While the cool climate partly explains the very existence of champagne it is also one of the keys to the wine's quality, for the Champagne region is France's most northerly vineyard, which makes it the perfect place to produce the thin, acid base wine from which to make top-quality fizz. The relatively high acidity in the grapes, a vital ingredient in champagne's long ageing, is naturally preserved by the slow ripening process this far north.

Champagne is able to age slowly and gracefully, adding nuances of flavour and complexity as it does so while still retaining a delightful freshness for many years. It is this quality which sets the top level of champagne production apart from even the best sparkling wines made elsewhere around the world.

Of course, champagne is not solely the result of a marginal climate. It is a magical combination of climate, chalky soil and hundreds of years of human endeavour – refining, adjusting and improving both vine cultivation and winemaking – that enables something unique to emerge in the bottle.

Not all champagne is great. There are literally thousands of producers and it is certainly not true that they all achieve the high level of quality that a connoisseur would rightly expect from a bottle of champagne. Over 350 million bottles can be made following a bountiful harvest and a large chunk of this is sold at the entry price level of between £10 and £12 bottle. If you judged champagne by the standard of the product in this price sector you may wonder what all the fuss is about.

However there are also a number of houses, cooperatives and individual growers who make wines that are really worthy of the name champagne. It is the very best of these which are highlighted in the chapters that follow. Typically, each producer makes a number of different champagnes but it is their most typical and finest products that are featured. Where a champagne is considered of particularly high quality, it has also been highlighted as a 'Le Snob Essential'.

This is not meant to be an exhaustive list but rather a personal selection drawn from more than two decades of visiting this fascinating region and tasting wines with the men and women that make them. Thanks to the generosity of the Champenois I have managed to sample many of the region's finest wines and a wide selection of the top vintages produced there over the past ten decades. I hope you will be able to use the tips and recommendations in this book to find some of your own ultimate champagne drinking experiences.

» Fundamentals

The production regions

The Champagne appellation extends 150 km north to south and nearly 120 km east to west. This is not one continuous stretch of vineyard, but rather various separate groupings, with five main production areas: Montagne de Reims; Vallée de la Marne; Côte des Blancs; Côte de Sézanne and the Côte des Bar. Although each one is strongly associated with a particular grape, because the soils and aspect are not identical across each area, pockets of all three main grape varieties (see page 13) are found in each.

The 319 villages in the Champagne area are quality-rated under a system known as the *Echelle des Crus*, literally 'ladder of growths', and given a classification between 100 and 80 per cent. Of these 258 are assessed between 80 and 89 per cent; 44 are *premiers crus*, between 90 and 99 per cent; and 17 *grands crus* villages, all rated 100 per cent. These 17 are all in the three best-known districts with nine in the Montagne de Reims, six in the Côte des Blancs and two in the Vallée de la Marne.

Montagne de Reims

This region is best known for black grapes; the reputations of the *grands crus* villages of Mailly, Verzenay, Verzy, Ambonnay and Bouzy are based on Pinot Noir. It is the most widely planted grape in the region, but there are areas where Pinot Meunier is more evident, and important pockets of Chardonnay. The differing microclimates, aspects and exposures of individual sites result in a large range of wine styles. The soil types may also vary, although all the *grands crus* are on the chalky bedrock for which Champagne is rightly famous.

Vallée de la Marne

The vineyards are located more on clayey, marly and sandy soils with pockets of alluvial river deposits and less chalk evident as you go west from Epernay. The majority of plantings are Pinot Meunier, which because of its late bud-break and early ripening is less vulnerable in this frost-prone valley. Meunier has a reputation as Champagne's workhorse grape, less refined than the other two, but is widely used by the major houses because its fruitiness and early development help soften their non-vintage blends, making them more approachable when young.

Côte des Blancs

The vineyards in this region are mostly on the purest form of chalky belemnite sub-soil, rich in minerals and trace elements. More than 95 per cent are planted with Chardonnay, and grapes from the four *grands crus* villages clustered in the centre of the Côte – Cramant, Avize, Oger and Le Mesnil-sur-Oger – are the most sought after and command the highest price. Not only do they help lift any blend they are added to, pure Côte des Blancs Chardonnay from any of these villages can produce wines of great intensity, minerality and longevity although they also tend to be somewhat austere in their youth.

Côte de Sézanne

The sub-soil is mostly clay and clayey silt with pockets of chalk. Like the Côte des Blancs it is mainly planted with Chardonnay (64 per cent) but around one-fifth is given over to Pinot Meunier. Thanks partly to the favourable south-easterly aspect, the wines tend to get riper and be more forward and fruitier than those in the Côte des Blancs, some would also say they are slightly more rustic and less fine. The area is rated 87 per cent for white grapes and 85 per cent for black grapes on the *Echelle des Crus*.

Côte des Bar

The vast majority of the area – some 83 per cent – is planted with Pinot Noir. Almost exactly half the appellation's Pinot Noir is planted in the Côte des Bar. This is the only place in France where wine may be produced under three different appellations, one fizzy (champagne) and two still (the red wines Rosé des Riceys and Coteaux Champenois).

Rare grape varieties

In addition to the three main grapes used to make champagne there are also about 100 hectares of four other varieties: Arbanne, Petit Meslier, Pinot Blanc and Pinot Gris. The latter two you might find elsewhere in Alsace or the New World but Petit Meslier and Arbanne are rarer, old Champagne varieties most often found in the Côte de Bars. Between them they make up less than 1 per cent of grapes planted. Traditionally they were harder to grow in the region, and so the main three came to dominate the vineyards.

Types of grape

There are several types of grape planted, but there are three main varieties used for champagne which account for just under 100 per cent of grapes planted, about 33,850 hectares in total.

Chardonnay

When the grapes are young, expect fresh, lifted citrus notes, plenty of crisp acidity and some floral aromas. Pure Côte des Blancs Chardonnay can have a flinty, mineral, chalky note on the palate, even iodine and a salty hint of the sea.

Pinot Noir

This grape variety brings more body, roundness and richness to a blend, and structure too. Pinot Noir from the north-facing Montagne de Reims *grands crus* often has a penetrating acidity, which makes it very long-lived.

Pinot Meunier

Often overtly fruity, the grapes may have a slightly rustic note, and some spiciness. Blends that use a high percentage of Meunier tend to develop more quickly. They are rarely used to produce a single-varietal champagne, though good examples most certainly exist.

Styles of champagne

Champagne is all designated either 'vintage' or 'non-vintage', but within these two parameters there are many variants of dryness, sweetness, style, quality and colour. The vast majority (at least four out of every five bottles of champagne sold) are classified as Brut Non-Vintage. The 'brut' part relates to the amount of residual sugar in the wine (the dosage levels) and can be anything between 0 to 15 grams per litre, but is typically between 10 and 12 grams.

The level of dosage in brut styles has gradually been coming down, following a decade or so of higher summer temperatures and longer sunshine hours, resulting in riper fruit. Average potential alcohol levels are up too. Stylistically there has also been growing interest in bone-dry 'extra brut' styles

Dosage levels in champagne

Level	Grams per litre
Brut Nature (or Zéro dosage)	0–2
Extra Brut	0–6
Brut	0–15
Extra Sec	12–20
Sec	17–35
Demi-sec	33–50
Doux	50+

and *non-dosé* champagnes, which have no sugar added at all when they are disgorged.

Non-vintage and vintage champagne

Non-vintage champagne is a blend of two or more harvests. Multi-vintage might be a better description, as these wines are typically made from one harvest year base plus reserve wine (see page 76) from two or more previous harvests (see 'Blending' on page 20).

Vintage champagne must be made 100 per cent from the year indicated on the label. It represents less than 5 per cent of champagne produced, and is only generally produced in years when the climate is particularly kind. Vintages are widely declared by a majority of producers perhaps three or four times a decade, but these are not necessarily evenly spaced out. For example, at the end of the 1980s, there were three high-class harvests one after another, in 1988, 1989 and 1990. There was then a gap until the classic 1995 vintage which was immediately followed by another great, but entirely different, style of vintage in 1996.

Blanc de Blancs

A Blanc de Blancs champagne is made entirely from white grapes. The vast majority will be all-Chardonnay, although there are other varieties, including Pinot Blanc, Arbane and Petit Meslier. A Blanc de Blancs style, especially one made from the *grands crus* villages of the Côte des Blancs like Avize or Le Mesnil-sur-Oger, may possess great ageing potential. When youthful, the style does tend to be unforthcoming and is often quite austere but it can develop toasty richness with age.

Blanc de Noirs

Literally, white wine made from black grapes, in the case of champagne it is made from either Pinot Noir or Pinot Meunier, or a blend of the two. It tends to be a richer, fuller style but good examples are not that easy to find, partly because few of the large houses make it. Two good producers that do are merchant house Drappier and grower Serge Mathieu, both of which are based in the Côte des Bar, where Pinot Noir is widely planted.

Rosé

Nearly all pink champagne is made by blending in a little red wine (between 5 and 20 per cent), which will also have been made in Champagne, with white champagne – the more red wine you use, the darker the hue of the rosé. In Europe, this method of making a rosé wine is only allowed within the Champagne appellation. Pink fizz may also be made by the *saignée* method, in which pigment to colour the wine is literally bled from the skins (most rosé table wine is made like this), but few producers use this method, partly because it is more difficult to do and control the resulting colour (one house that does is Laurent-Perrier). Some smaller producers these days use a combination of the two methods.

Partly because better, softer and fruitier styles are now being made more widely, rosé champagne has been the fastest growing sector of the champagne market over the past few years since the millennium. Unvintaged rosé champagne is invariably more expensive than its white counterparts and is often priced at a similar level to vintage champagne.

Prestige Cuvée

Most producers, large and small, make a wine that they would put in this category. Typically the top of the range, usually the most expensive and often specially packaged, this will be their effort to produce the best, most impressive champagne from the grapes they have access to. In some respects this sector is defined by champagne's icon brands – Dom Pérignon, Cristal and Krug – but other top producers make wines of similar quality and complexity.

Single-vineyard wines

Most champagne is made by blending together grapes from different vineyards (see page 20), but in recent years interest has grown in wines made from grapes picked on individual sites that have been found over the years to produce something special. These may be walled vineyards, or *clos*. The most obvious example of this is Philipponnat's vertiginous, south-facing Clos des Goisses in the highly rated 99 per cent *premier cru* village of Mareuil-sur-Ay. The wines from Clos des Goisses reflect the perfect exposure of this site and are certainly as worthy of attention as other more widely famous single vineyard champagnes like Krug's Clos de Mesnil and Clos d'Ambonnay.

New single-vineyard wines are coming onto the market all the time as winemakers learn more about the individual sites they use, partly through the wider practice of keeping wines with an interesting character for longer before the blending process.

» Malolactic fermentation

In between the two stages of fermentation, before
bottling, most champagne will also go through
malolactic fermentation, a biochemical process
involving various bacteria that transforms harsh
malic acid into softer lactic acid. The majority of
producers encourage this process (by keeping the
wine warm or introducing the lactic bacteria), as it
softens the wines and makes them more
approachable and less acidic tasting in their youth.

However certain producers, including Krug,
Lanson, Gosset, Bollinger and Louis Roederer,
choose not to put their wines through malolactic
fermentation for stylistic reasons. Their wines will
therefore tend to taste fresher or, because they take
more time to mature, be released after longer ageing.
The effect of blocking the 'malo' is easiest to see in
Lanson's non-vintage cuvée Black Label, because it
doesn't use any oak in the winemaking process, so
oaky flavours won't mask the difference.

Blending

Whether it is non-vintage wine, vintaged or a special cuvée, the majority of champagne is a blend (*assemblage*). A blend of several harvests (apart from vintage), of grape varieties, and of the myriad of different *crus* and vineyards across the appellation.

Blends vs single vineyard

With nearly every other fine wine in Europe, vintage is considered the best, and initially, champagne was no different, but the quality was very inconsistent in this northerly vineyard. The practice of blending was started to combat the inadequacies of a particular year, and promote regularity of style and quality.

Blending is also used to help bring complexity and finesse to the top vintage and prestige styles. The word 'cuvée' refers to a specific champagne blend (as well as the juice from the first pressing.). The idea is that blending will result in a more complete wine, one that has more different facets, greater complexity, additional nuances of aroma and flavour. In short it will be a better, more interesting wine.

Many Champenois (people from Champagne) are convinced that great champagne comes only from blending together different component parts and however interesting single vineyard or single varietal wines (those made from just one grape variety) may be, they will never reach the heights achieved by Champagne's greatest blends.

Champagne production

The production process starts with the grape harvest (vendage), typically in mid-September. In Champagne the grapes are all picked by hand; mechanical harvesting is not allowed because it is important not to break the skins before pressing. Whole bunches of grapes are collected in small crates to avoid crushing and delivered quickly to the press house.

Pressing

The grapes are then pressed as gently and as quickly as possible, typically still in the traditional *coquard* basket press, although many producers now use pneumatic presses. The juice from the 4,000 kilos of grapes that makes up the *marc* in a standard size press is separated as it runs off during the pressing process. The cuvée, the best quality, clearer free run juice produced at the start of the pressing is kept separate from the darker *taille* which contains more impurities as a result of the greater pressure gradually exerted in the press. The amount of juice that is drawn off in the *cuvée* and the *taille* is strictly regulated (2,050 litres and 500 litres respectively).

Before the first alcoholic fermentation takes place, impurities in the pressed grape juice are removed by *débourbage*, a processing of settling that allows solid particles to sink to the bottom of the vat, therefore enabling clear juice to be drawn off at the top. This filtration process may be encouraged by chilling the juice in the vat.

Primary fermentation

The clear juice then goes through alcoholic fermentation, in which the natural sugar in the grapes is converted into alcohol while the resultant carbon dioxide is allowed to escape. This produces the base wine. Most often this stage takes place in large stainless-steel vats, although a few famous houses and an increasing band of smaller producers ferment the wines wholly or partially in oak barrels or casks of varying sizes.

At the end of this process the producer will have a collection of still wines (*vins clairs*), perhaps more than 200 in the case of some of the larger houses. From these they will make their blends for all the different cuvées they produce in any given year, and they may also hold back quantities of these still wines to use as reserve wines for subsequent years (see page 76).

Secondary fermentation

Once a blend is complete, it is put in a bottle, the *liqueur de tirage* (a solution of wine, yeast and sugar) is added and the bottles are laid on their side in a cool cellar. The secondary fermentation now takes place slowly in the bottle, during which the bubbles are created (the *prise de mousse*) as the carbon dioxide given off is trapped inside. The wine will then be left to age on its lees (the deposits of residual yeast) for a minimum of 15 months, in the case of non-vintage, or three years for vintage champagne.

Riddling

The last stage in the fermentation process is *remuage*, or riddling, the method of removing the yeast deposits left in the bottle. Traditionally this was done by hand, and took about six to eight weeks, but now it mostly takes place in a computer-programmed gyropalette machine. The bottles are placed in the machine and are twisted, shaken and turned at certain intervals over a few days, eventually finishing in a vertical position, neck down in a wooden container (the *pupitres*), with the yeast deposit settled on the crown cap or cork closure.

Disgorging

The bottles are then ready for the *dégorgement* (disgorging) process, to remove the yeast deposits. The neck of the bottle is frozen, and the cap or cork is removed. Under the pressure that has built up during the fermentation process, a pellet of semi-frozen liquid containing the yeast deposit shoots out. (See pages 49 and 71 for further information.)

Sugar levels

After the *dégorgement* process, the bottle is topped up and the *liqueur de dosage* is added – the amount of sugar added varies depending on the style of champagne being made (see page 14 for the differing dosage levels). The wine is then returned to the cellar to rest and allow the dosage to marry, ideally at least for several months, after which it is then ready to go on sale.

The champagne industry

The champagne industry is a complex collection of different producers, generally divided into merchant houses known as *négociant-manipulants* (NM), growers known as *récoltant-manipulants* (RM), and cooperatives, *coopérative-manipulants* (CM). The initials NM, RM and CM appear in front of a short number on the label of all champagnes telling you which group has produced any given bottle.

Merchant houses

There are 293 *négociant* houses, the largest of which own the dozen or so major brands that dominate worldwide sales of champagne and include the best-known names like Moët & Chandon, Veuve Clicquot, Laurent-Perrier, GH Mumm, Piper Heidsieck, Taittinger, Lanson and Bollinger.

Although the large *négociant* houses dominate sales of champagne, particularly those outside France, collectively they own only a tenth of Champagne's total vineyard area. The bulk of Champagne's grapes come from the growers who between them farm 90 per cent of the appellation's 33,077 hectares that are in active production. For example, Champagne's largest group, Louis Vuitton Moët Hennessy (LVMH), has the biggest total vineyard holding among the *négociants*, with some 1,684 hectares. Howver, this area provides less than one-third of the grapes they'd need to produce their six brands of champagne (Moët & Chandon, Dom Pérignon, Mercier, Ruinart, Veuve Clicquot

Ponsardin and Krug), over 55 million bottles of which are sold each year. To make up the difference they need to buy in the production of around another 4,000 hectares from across the appellation.

To fuel their brands, most of the big producers have to buy in the majority of the grapes they need from literally dozens of different growers and co-ops. Houses like Louis Roederer and Bollinger, which both own enough vineyards to supply about two-thirds of their grape requirements, are rarities.

Growers and co-ops

Of the 15,628 growers currently operating in Champagne, over two-thirds just sell their grapes to the *négociants*. Only around 2,000 make and sell wine under their own name.

Many growers have joined forces to form local cooperatives to provide them with central services like pressing the grapes, bottling, even marketing and selling the wine. The cooperatives may also sell grapes and wine on behalf of their grower members to the major *négociant* houses. Out of the 137 cooperatives operating, only 66 actually sell finished wine themselves and 32 of these export their produce but some make high-quality champagne.

Some smaller cooperative groups have banded together to form 'super co-ops', the two largest of which now own significant marques of their own in the shape of Nicolas Feuillatte and Jacquart; the former recently became the fifth largest selling champagne on the market.

Bottle sizes

Champagne comes in bottle sizes all the way up to the staggeringly large 50-litre Murgatroyd. Most are limited to the sizes below, standard and Magnum being the most common. Larger bottles are rare and mostly for special marketing purposes for special occasions or special cuvées, and are only available from certain producers, such as the 27-litre Primat bottles, offered exclusively by Drappier.

Half 37.5 cl ½ bottle

Standard 0.75 litre 1

Magnum 1.5 litres 2

Jeroboam 3 litres 4

Methuselah 6 litres 8

Salmanazar 9 litres 12

Balthazar 12 litres 16

Nebuchadnezzar 15 litres 20

Tasting techniques

When you are tasting champagne with the idea of analysing it, as opposed to drinking it simply for hedonistic pleasure, you probably want the bottle to be slightly less chilled. Over-chilling will dampen down the aromas, cellar temperature of about 10–12°C is better than 7–8°C, although the cooler temperature is better for the slow release of the mousse (the stream of fine bubbles that float gently to the surface of the glass). Fill the glass to less than halfway, perhaps around one-third is ideal, enough to be able to assess the mousse and more importantly give plenty of room for the aromas to gather.

Observe the colour

You can learn something from the colour of the wine, which may vary from the palest lemon or straw in youth to old gold in maturity. Almost colourless suggests a young champagne or perhaps a Blanc de Blancs style. Something moving towards light yellow may indicate more maturity or perhaps a riper vintage. Blends with more Pinot in them also tend to be darker and a Blancs de Noirs may have a hint of pink in it. A fully mature vintage champagne aged for a decade or more will often take on a rich, golden hue. Rosé champagnes may range in intensity from the merest hint of colour (sometimes called partridge eye) right through to opal or copper and on to a light ruby red that might be mistaken for a glass of Beaujolais.

Bubbles

It is often said that a steady, persistent stream of fine, small bubbles (the mousse) is a sign of quality in champagne. However in truth the speed, persistence and size of the bubbles is more likely to be effected by the type of glass you use and its cleanliness than a clear sign of inherent quality. You can, however, assess the mousse reasonably accurately on tasting: the smaller the bubbles the smoother the mousse feels in the mouth. The tiniest bubbles help create a creamy silky texture on the finish.

Aromas

As for champagne's aromas we can perhaps helpfully put them into several groups.

Floral aromas: lime blossom, violet, orange blossom, hawthorn.

Fruity aromas: citrus ones like lemon, grapefruit, lime, orange; yellow fruit such as peach, apricot, nectarine and quince; exotic fruit including mango, banana, coconut and lychees; plus red or black fruit like raspberry, strawberry, blackcurrant, plum.

Vegetal aromas: fresh almonds, cut grass, truffle.

Dried fruit aromas: hazelnuts, raisins, dried figs.

Epicurean aromas: brioche, vanilla, butter, toast, biscuit notes, honey, gingerbread, candied fruit, mocha, white chocolate, mushroom, smoke, spices like cinnamon, notes of decay and torrefaction.

While it is possible to generalise about the typical flavours that each of the three main grape varieties tend to bring to a champagne blend, it is also worth pointing out that you are likely to come across exceptions to the rule.

Words from the wise

Simon Field Champagne buyer,
Berry Bros & Rudd, London

» Magnum force

Champagne comes in a bewildering array of bottle
sizes, from the somewhat perfunctory quarter bottle,
all the way up to the Nebuchadnezzar and beyond.
The larger the size the more impractical the vessel –
A Melchizedek is a 30-litre bottle, and in addition to
being fantastically impractical (unless one has a
small crane to hand) is also bound to be of inferior
quality, as the liquid has been decanted from a series
of smaller bottles, post ageing, and will have lost
freshness and fizz in the process. This process,
known as transvasage, is practised on all bottles
above jeroboam size.

A magnum, however, allows champagne to age
most gracefully and to maintain the fundamental
tension between acidity, sugar, fruit and fizz which
make this region so famous. It's all to do, they say,
with the rate of oxidation and the relative surface
area of liquid exposed to the air. For me, though it's
a matter of taste alone.

Palate

Our sense of smell is infinitely more developed than our sense of taste. Humans can identify four taste flavours: saltiness, sweetness, acidity and bitterness. Some would add umami, which has long fascinated experimental chefs like Heston Blumenthal and also strikes a note with some of champagne's top winemakers including Dom Pérignon's Chef de Cave, Richard Geoffroy.

When you are tasting champagne you are looking at the initial 'attack', the crispness, freshness and zip, the balance of fruit and acidity, and the feeling or mouth texture you experience partly effected by the mousse and the fizziness of the wine. Look then for the wine's structure and intensity: is it light, delicate, ethereal or perhaps rich, full-bodied and structured? Is it nicely balanced, rounded, smooth and harmonious? Is the palate texture creamy and silky smooth or edgy, sharp, even aggressive? What about the maturity, does it have those yeasty bready autolytic characters of fine aged champagne, is there any hint of oak or of slow oxidation. Finally does it show many of these facets together, plus a complex array of attractive flavours and aromas with a finish that stays in your mouth for a long time? If it does this suggests real class.

» International marques

Dominant exporters

There are currently 297 *négociant* houses operating in Champagne, 232 of which exported wine to markets outside France in 2009 and between them they accounted for nearly 87 per cent of all export sales. The largest three brands between them – Moët & Chandon, Veuve Clicquot and GH Mumm – shipped a third of the *négociants* total exports.

The largest houses tend to have their cellars based either in Reims or Epernay, although their physical location doesn't tell us much about the style of wine they produce, as these larger *négociants* buy in grapes from growers spread all over the region.

Reims

Ruinart

4, Rue des Crayères, 51100 Reims

Tel: +33 (0)3 26 77 51 51 www.ruinart.com

Ruinart was founded by Nicolas Ruinart in 1729, and is the oldest producer of champagne still operating today. Ruinart is part of the LVMH group, but its wines are still relatively unknown outside France. It is particularly renowned for its Blanc de Blancs, all-Chardonnay styles, which reach a fabulous peak in the vintage prestige cuvée Dom Ruinart. Its pink counterpart – Dom Ruinart Rosé – is the most expensive and exclusive line in the present range. The Dom Ruinart wines tend to improve with a little further aging after release. They are essentially food wines that work very well with white meats, veal and feathered game.

» Dom Ruinart Blanc de Blancs 1998

Unusually, and unlike most great all-Chardonnay champagnes, the grapes used for this champagne don't come solely from *grands crus* villages in the Côte des Blancs. A third comes from the Montagne de Reims villages of Sillery, Puislieux, Verzenay and Mailly. Pale gold in colour with developed aromas of brioche and toast, this wine seems rich, ripe and forward, as most vintage cuvées from the warm 1998 harvest tend to be, but it hasn't yet reached its peak.

» Dom Ruinart Rosé 1996

A rich coppery pink, Dom Ruinart Rosé tends to be launched a year or so later than its white counterpart, but despite that this wine is still extraordinarily youthful. Again, it is Chardonnay-driven with no black grapes in the blend, just the addition of between 15 per cent and 20 per cent red wine, all *grand cru* Pinot Noir Bouzy Rouge.

Lanson

66, Rue de Courlancy, 51100 Reims

Tel: +33 (0)3 26 78 50 50 www.lanson.com

This famous house has just celebrated its 250th anniversary. Since being purchased by the Boizel Chanoine group in 2006, the wines have improved and it looks poised to return to its former glories. Lanson's strength is its vintage Gold Label wines, which after a more difficult period *sans vineyards* in the early nineties (when the brand name was sold on without the vineyards), has returned to impressive form with the 1998 and especially the 1999 releases.

» **Lanson (Gold Label) Vintage 1999**
The current vintage release Gold Label Brut Vintage 1999 is on impressively good form after a decade of ageing gracefully. It has a nicely developed biscuity note and silky intensity.

» **Lanson Noble Cuvée Brut Vintage 1998**
This is the original Noble Cuvée prestige style (there are now three), usually a classy, nicely balanced, understated ratio of 70:30 Chardonnay/Pinot Noir blend. Because it is not that well known it's great value too. Very fresh, lively sherbetty fizz with an attractive waxy, creamy, palate texture building this still has long future ahead of it.

Veuve Clicquot Ponsardin

1, Place des Droits de l'Homme, 51100 Reims

Tel: +33 (0)3 26 89 53 90 www.veuve-clicquot.com

Veuve Clicquot is perhaps the most successful house in terms of creating the right image. It is certainly the brand most admired by other large producers. The downside of the iconic status that the Yellow Label non-vintage cuvée has acquired is that the volume has shot up and it is hard to keep quality consistently high when producing over 15 million bottles a year. The full-bodied Pinot Noir-dominated house style can best be seen in the fine vintage releases over the past few decades, which also age extremely well.

Words from the wise

Didier Mariotti Chef de Cave,
GH Mumm, Reims

» The correct temperature

Champagne is a wine even though it's also a sparkling wine. I think people always serve champagne too cold and, just as with white table wine, this will emphasise the freshness. As with other wines we have to select the right temperature and the best glass according to the blend – we don't use the same glass for red Burgundy and red Bordeaux.

When it comes to our prestige cuvée R Lalou, for example, which is a blend of roughly equal parts of Chardonnay and Pinot Noir, it depends which side of the blend you want to emphasise. The side I prefer depends on the time of day, on my mood and the drinking occasion – as an aperitif or paired with food and what kind. The temperature I drink it at and the glass I use depends on these factors. A cooler temperature (8–10°C) will emphasise the Chardonnay in the blend, while a warmer temperature (14°C) will show the Pinot Noir side.

>> **Veuve Clicquot Brut Vintage Réserve (2002)**
Originally launched in September 2007, this wine is
still available and has developed very attractively. A
blend dominated by black grapes (60 per cent Pinot
Noir, 7 per cent Pinot Meunier), it gives a rounded
and rich, full-bodied style that's now showing a
creamy palate with distinctive biscuity notes and
good mouthfeel. It will develop further complexity
for perhaps another decade.

>> **Veuve Clicquot Cave Privée Rosé 1989**
Le Snob ESSENTIAL From a ripe year, with lower acidity, this
pale copper pink 1989 rosé was a
vintage that many houses predicted wouldn't last
that long, but this rosé remains remarkably fresh.
There are roasted coffee, mocha notes, strawberry
fruit on the initial palate then a meaty, savoury mid-
palate and a long finish.

>> **Veuve Clicquot La Grande Dame 1998**
Luxury cuvée La Grande Dame is less vinous and
more elegant than the meaty Vintage Réserve style
thanks to larger amounts of Chardonnay in the
blend (around 40 per cent) and the fact that it is
solely Blanc de Blancs *grand cru*.

Louis Roederer

21, Boulevard Lundy, 51053 Reims

Tel: +33 (0)3 26 40 42 11
www.champagne-roederer.com

One of the most celebrated houses in Champagne,
and still entirely owned by the Rouzaud family,
Roederer's wines are particularly renowned for
their elegance and finesse. The quality of the range

is partly due to the highly rated 218-hectare vineyard estate, much of it located in the best *grands crus*, which supplies about two-thirds of their grape needs.

» Louis Roederer Brut Premier NV

This is a particularly fine non-vintage cuvée. It's an elegant, complex style with finesse and structure that's underpinned by the use of reserve wines from three different harvests, which are matured in oak casks for three to five years. It is aged for 40 months before release, but like other top-quality non-vintage you could cellar it for a couple of years more.

» Louis Roederer Cristal 2002

Le Snob ESSENTIAL Originally created exclusively for Tsar Alexander II of Russia in 1876, prestige cuvée Cristal, in its clear bottle and gold cellophane wrap, is one of the wines that defines this luxury sector of the market (along with Krug and Dom Pérignon), and is perhaps the most sought after in the appellation. It is a subtle yet complex wine that's all about balance: balancing flavours, mouthfeel and fine acidity. Its power and intensity are disguised by a seductive, silky, textural cloak. Initially attractive on release, with good cellaring the wine will develop layers of complexity over several years.

» **Louis Roederer Blanc de Blancs Vintage 2004**
Half the price of Cristal but not half the quality, this is very pale, intense, startlingly fresh and linear in its youth. With time it develops into one of the most delightful wines in the range.

GH Mumm

29, Rue du Champ de Mars, 51100 Reims

Tel: + 33 (0)3 26 49 59 69 www.mumm.com

After a difficult period, and several changes of ownership, GH Mumm's range continues to show steady improvement under the management of Pernod Ricard, a trend set in train by winemaker Dominique Demarville (now at Veuve Clicquot) and carried on by his successor Didier Mariotti.

UNIQUE » RARE » LITTLE-KNOWN » ULTIMATE **Snob**

Limited editions Louis Roederer has released a limited number of methuselahs of Cristal from the celebrated 2002 vintage, which, if you can find one will set you back about £10,000. Roederer has only made methuselahs of Cristal once before, with the fine 1990 vintage that was released for the millennium in 1999. These now fetch in the region of £35,000.

>> **Mumm de Cramant**

This very pale, delicate, fresh all-Chardonnay cuvée is made at a lower pressure in the *crémant* style (see page 95; it used to be named Crémant de Cramant) which gives it a softer texture in the mouth. It is actually made from one vintage but, because it is designed to be consumed while crisp and young, it doesn't have a year on the label – by law vintage styles have to be aged for a minimum of three years before release.

>> **R Lalou 1998**

Mumm's prestige cuvée René Lalou was discontinued at the end of the eighties, but its natural successor R Lalou, made from the 1998 vintage, was first released in 2007 and is based on the same company-owned vineyard parcels. An elegant wine with an initial emphasis on citrus fruits, the freshness from the north-facing slopes of Verzy and Verzenay is still noticeable, and the wine has more ageing capacity yet. The excellent 1999 vintage was also released in early 2011.

Charles Heidsieck

12, Allée du Vignoble, 51100 Reims

Tel: +33 (0)3 26 84 43 50
www.charlesheidsieck.com

There are three brands in Champagne with the name Heidsieck but Charles Heidsieck, the youngest, is the one to look for if you are hunting out top-quality wines right across the range. Established by Charles-Camille Heidsieck, the firm was bought by what is now the Rémy-Cointreau group in 1985.

They kept on winemaker Daniel Thibault, widely viewed as the best of his generation, with a remit to make Charles Heidsieck Brut Réserve a top-class cuvée. This and other Charles Heidsieck wines have gone on to win numerous awards and happily his successor, Régis Camus, is continuing in the same award-winning ways.

» Charles Heidsieck Brut Réserve NV

Le Snob ESSENTIAL The secret behind Thibault's success in creating this cuvée was in using large quantities of quality reserve wines in each blend (up to 40 per cent) which is double what most houses typically use, and then in aging these very fine blends for longer before release. The current release is based on the 2005 harvest and has 40 per cent reserve wine of between two and ten years old in the blend. There are notes of fresh-baked bread and ripe peachy fruit, a sherbetty lift and then an intensely creamy soft mid-palate and long finish.

» Charles Heidsieck Blanc des Millénaires 1995

Exclusively composed of Chardonnay from the Côte des Blancs, this magical wine from the great '95 vintage is at a glorious peak of maturity. Ripe and opulent on the nose, with notes of marzipan, hazelnuts and white chocolate, the palate is rich, creamy and silky; a delight.

» Charles Heidsieck Brut Vintage 2000

This vintage champagne really is only made in the best years – '96, '95and '90 precede it. At first release, in late 2007, although it showed lovely balance and rich texture, it only gave a hint of the glories to come in maturity. Now, a burnished gold colour, it has opened up, the palate texture has softened with notes of vanilla and mocha starting to develop.

» **Charles Heidsieck Brut Rosé NV**
The first cuvée of this wine was released at the end of 2008. A soft, deliciously fruity, beautifully balanced, creamy textured champagne, it is a worthy partner to Charles Heidsieck Brut Réserve, which has been one of the best and most consistent non-vintage cuvées on the market for the past 15 years.

Taittinger

9, Place Saint-Nicaise, 51100 Reims

Tel: +33 (0)3 26 85 45 35 www.taittinger.com

Founded in 1931, Pierre-Emmanuel Taittinger is the latest family member to run this famous house, whose 228 hectares of vineyard (including holdings in six *grands crus* in the Côte des Blancs) provides a significant proportion of its needs. Chardonnay plays an important part in the range and reaches a high point, in the prestige cuvée Comtes de Champagne Blanc de Blancs.

» **Comtes de Champagne Blanc de Blancs 1998**

Le Snob ESSENTIAL An all-Chardonnay cuvée that really needs more than a decade to show its true colours and lush palate. It works particularly well in riper vintages. This example is classy and already showing an attractive biscuity note and silken texture, but it will get better still.

>> **Prélude Grands Crus NV**
An award winning 50/50 blend of Chardonnay from the top-rated vineyards of Avize and Le Mesnil-sur-Oger, and Pinot Noir from Bouzy and Ambonnay, which with extra aging shows a rich, mellow fullness and a satisfyingly long finish.

Epernay

Moët & Chandon

20, Avenue de Champagne, 51200 Epernay

Tel: +33 (0)3 26 51 20 20 www.moet.com

Given that Moët Brut Impérial is the top-selling champagne worldwide and is produced in very large quantities (close to 30 million bottles a year) the quality is impressively consistent and always seems to go up a notch in magnum. Moët's vintage wines (called Grand Vintage) are quite a step up and in top years like 1988, 1990 and 1995 represent one of the best bargains in champagne.

>> **Moët & Chandon Grand Vintage Brut 2002**
This wine is made in what looks likely to be judged the best vintage of this decade. Moët released it out of sequence after the 2003 version and now plans to age all vintage releases seven years in the cellar rather than five, according to Chef de Cave Benoît

Gouez. The blend of Grand Vintage 2002 is 51 per cent Chardonnay, 26 per cent Pinot Noir and 23 per cent Pinot Meunier. Initially it shows ripe stone fruit aromas with notes of fresh brioche. Fine balancing acidity suggests it has a long future and will develop attractively gathering more complexity.

Dom Pérignon

www.domperignon.com

Owned by Moët, but with a separate winemaking team led by Chef de Cave Richard Geoffroy since 1990, this is the original prestige cuvée champagne. Although it is usually first released seven years after the harvest from which it was made, if you consume it immediately, as sadly the majority of consumers do, you will be missing much of the point of the wine, as its flavours and complexity develop only gradually over time. Try to give it at least three or four years extra cellaring. In recognition of the wine's slow development, Moët re-releases the wine twice under the Oenothèque Collection at around 12 and 20-plus years in what Geoffroy calls its second and third 'plenitude'.

» **Dom Pérignon 2000**
Chief winemaker Richard Geoffroy describes this as a 'paradoxical vintage: fresh yet mature, austere but seductive' and it does seem quite opulent and forward as an aperitif, but the minute you put food with it the underlying acidity that will give it a very long life comes to the fore.

›› Stages of ageing

Good champagne, particularly vintage, ages very
well and typically goes through several phases of
development from zingy, fresh and fruity through to
tertiary notes like chocolate, mushroom and leather.
At Dom Pérignon, for example, Chef de Cave
Richard Geoffroy releases his wines at three optimal
moments: the first after seven years of ageing, the
second at 12 to 15 years, the third after two decades.

The aromas change dramatically, initially tending
towards notes of fresh brioche, citrus fruits, sweet
spices and occasionally honey. The second stage
extends to classic characteristics of maturity: aromas
of toast, hazelnuts, biscuits, malt, chocolate and
spices. Beyond 20 years, the aromatic range takes on
a new dimension and becomes more exotic and
intriguing, veering from the classic path to evoke
unusual sensations, almost like perfume:
sandalwood, musk, new leather, a blend of oriental
spices, blond tobacco and white truffles.

» **Dom Pérignon Oenothèque 1995**

Oenothèque 1995 and 1975 are a particularly impressive pair. The former, disgorged in February 2007, will continue to open up but is already very rich and lush with some ripe mango fruit and a creamy vanilla palate, although there's still plenty of freshness to give it balance.

» **Dom Pérignon Oenothèque 1975**

The 1975 has an altogether more perfumed, honeyed, floral nose and a meaty, savoury intensity. It's not big and powerful but subtle and complex. It

UNIQUE » RARE » LITTLE-KNOWN » ULTIMATE **Snob**

Bespoke cuvée In the summer of 2008, Perrier-Jouët Belle released Epoque Blanc de Blancs 2000 'By and For', which cost £35,000 for a case of 12 bottles. Just 100 cases of this 'bespoke' cuvée were offered worldwide and only to customers in the USA, Britain, Japan, China, Russia, Switzerland and France. As part of the package they meet up with Chef de Cave Hervé Deschamps at Perrier-Jouët's Maison Belle Epoque in the Avenue de Champagne to customise their wine to their own personal taste. This involves, after tasting the various options available, picking the exact dosage to be used in the *liqueur d'expedition* added after the wine is disgorged and before it is given its final cork.

demonstrates dramatically what those who drink the 2000 quickly may be missing.

Perrier-Jouët

28, Avenue de Champagne, 51200 Epernay

Tel: +33 (0)3 26 53 38 00 www.perrier-jouet.com

Perrier-Jouët is best known for the Art Nouveau flower motif (designed by Emile Gallé) that adorns its prestige cuvée Belle Epoque, arguably the most distinctive bottle in champagne. Now reaping the benefit of Pernod Ricard's investment, Perrier-Jouët's range is proving more consistent with the straight vintage and Blason Rosé, the best buys, while Belle Epoque has been on good form since the mid-nineties.

>> ### Perrier-Jouët Belle Epoque Brut 2002

At the launch of this cuvée from the top class 2002 vintage everyone was surprised about how lush, forward and hedonistically seductive the wine immediately seemed and some have doubted its staying power, although ripe vintages like '76 and '89 often have remarkable longevity. Older vintages of Belle Epoque ('98, '96 and '95) in bottle, magnum and jeroboam sizes offer delightful complexity.

>> **Perrier-Jouët Blason Rosé NV**

This exuberantly fruity and stylish rosé is not at all well known yet often seems more attractive than the pink Belle Epoque. It's full of primary red berry fruit, with quite a soft creamy palate but enough acidity to keep it fresh.

Pol Roger

1, Rue Henri Lelarge, 51206 Epernay

Tel: +33 (0)3 26 59 58 00 www.polroger.com

Pol Roger was Winston Churchill's favourite brand of champagne. Over the last decade, the company has re-invested in improved production facilities, employed Krug's former winemaker, Dominique Petit, and gained access to more high-quality *grand cru* fruit. As a result, all of its wines have been showing consistently well, not just the excellent long-lived vintage styles which have always been the strength of this house.

>> **Pol Roger Brut Réserve**

A soft and attractively powerful three-way blend of Chardonnay and Pinots Noir and Meunier. Extra lees aging (see page 44) before release – the current cuvee is based on the 2006 harvest with reserve wine from '05 and '04 – help rich, ripe, yeasty aromas develop.

>> **Pol Roger Brut Vintage 2000**

This rich and full bodied style, as usual a 60/40 blend of Pinot Noir and Chardonnay, has fragrant, perfumed fruit while the palate is rich, yet fine-grained with a lovely concentration. There's a hint of spice with an attractive biscuity note before a long finish.

Pol Roger Blanc de Chardonnay 1999

This is a superb all-Chardonnay vintage champagne capable of long ageing and able to stand up to quite robust food. Tasted in magnum, it is still incredibly fresh with a very lifted grapefruit acidity but also a creamy texture developing – this is one to put away for two or three years at least.

Pol Roger Cuvée Sir Winston Churchill 1998

Le Snob ESSENTIAL The family is curiously reticent about the exact make-up of this celebrated cuvée. Initially it has attractive notes of brioche, toasted almonds and ripe stone fruit with a luscious fleshy texture tempered by fine acidity. It's a big, full-bodied, gloriously rich wine.

Recently Disgorged (RD)

RD is a concept which was first developed by Madame Lily Bollinger to show off the exceptional aging capabilities of Bollinger's wines with the 1952 vintage (released in 1961). RD is the Grande Année blend kept longer on it lees to heighten its aromatics. At disgorgement the wine gets a lighter dosage of between 3 and 4 g/l and is then released after three months so those that want a fresher style can drink it soon after disgorgement. RD is a Bollinger trademark so other houses use terms like 'late disgorgement' or *dégorgement tardive*.

Other regions

Bollinger

16, Rue Jules Lobet 51160 Aÿ

Tel: +33 (0)3 26 53 33 66
www.champagne-bollinger.com

This deeply traditional, family-run house based in the *grand cru* village of Ay, controls a 163-hectare vineyard estate that supplies two-thirds of its grape needs. Bollinger's commitment to the highest production standards was set out in its Charter of Ethics and Quality, published in 1992, the stringent rules of which have become a blueprint for quality in the region. All the Bollinger wines gather richness and complexity as they age, particularly the vintage.

» **Bollinger Special Cuvée**

On great form, the weighty, complex style is rich with a long finish but has shown increasing elegance as well as power. One of the top five NV cuvées in terms of consistency and quality, the current wine is a blend of 45 per cent 2006 harvest, 45 per cent from the 2005 harvest, and 10 per cent of an older reserve wine, some of which may date back 15 to 20 years.

» **Bollinger La Grande Année Rosé 1999**

It is hard to find a more beautifully balanced vintage rosé with raspberry fruit, creamy texture, charm and elegance. The 2002 is also a class act, but still quite linear and needs a few more years to develop, while the '99 will provide great drinking pleasure for several years now.

Words from the wise

Roger Jones Owner, The Harrow, Wiltshire

» Further ageing

I am keen to lay down certain multi-vintage champagne for further ageing, not just single-vintage – but it has to be the right wine to warrant this treatment, for example Krug Grande Cuvée, Gosset Grande Réserve and Jacquesson Cuvée 733, because these all offer fantastic value and do improve considerably with more time in bottle. Our experienced champagne-drinking clientele do appreciate the difference they see in the glass.

Don't be hesitant of buying older vintage wines like 1996, which can age terrifically. With vintage champagne you don't have to pay much more to get a wine that has already been aged considerably longer before you buy it. Veuve Clicquot Vintage Réserve (currently 2002) only costs about 30 per cent more than their non-vintage. On first release Dom Pérignon tends to need a few years before it starts to develop but it is definitely well worth the wait.

» Bollinger La Grande Année 2000 (and 2002)

Le Snob ESSENTIAL One of the best examples of what has turned out to be a very attractive, generally soft, ripe and forward-drinking vintage. And this wine is hardly on its last legs and in magnum has a long future ahead of it. Typical yeasty, autolytic notes, with more than a hint of Marmite, preface a soft, buttery, weighty palate, though there is nothing clumsy here, just vinous pleasure. The beautifully refined, balanced, more classical 2002 Grand Année, potentially a very long keeper, will follow.

Laurent-Perrier

Domaine Laurent-Perrier, 51150 Tours-sur-Marne

Tel: +33 (0)3 26 58 91 22 www.laurentperrier.com

Laurent-Perrier is probably still best known for its trend-setting non-vintage rosé, packaged in a distinctive bottle that kick-started the popularity of pink champagne. The company also boasts the most widely available *non-dosé* (bone-dry) style of champagne in Ultra Brut. Given the large number of such wines now being made, Laurent-Perrier may claim to have started another significant trend.

>> **Laurent-Perrier Brut NV**

This has a soft, moreish, light, delicate style with no harsh edges. It is easy to drink and expertly made, designed to leave you wanting more, not aiming to be too characterful.

>> **Grand Siècle La Cuvée NV**

This prestige cuvée is unusual in being a blend of three different harvests – the current version is based on 1999, 1997 and 1996 harvests, as well as a roughly 50/50 blend of Chardonnay and Pinot Noir. Subtle and delicate, not at all muscular, it tends to go buttery rather that toasty and yeasty with more age.

>> **Grand Siècle Cuvée Alexandra Rosé Vintage 1998**

A gorgeous coppery pink, heady floral scents and raspberry fruit develop into richer black fruit with a little time in the glass. This is a classic, elegant rosé, delicate but persistent and with great finesse. A luxurious indulgence.

053

Duval-Leroy

69, Avenue de Bammental, 51130 Vertus

Tel: +33 (0)3 26 52 10 75 www.duval-leroy.com

Carol Duval runs this excellent but underrated family-owned house, based in the village of Vertus in the Côte des Blancs. The quality of its vintage cuvées is built around the 200 hectares of prime vineyards it owns, which are mostly planted with Chardonnay. It has shown considerable innovation over the past decade releasing a string of interesting wines under its Authentis range.

Blanc de Chardonnay Brut Vintage 1999

A rich, golden yellow gives a hint of ripe, succulent fruit to follow, in this attractively mature vintage that offers very enjoyable drinking now.

Clos des Bouveries 2004

Part of the Authentis range, this is a single-vineyard, all-Chardonnay cuvée that comes from a low-yielding 3.5 hectare plot at the southern end of the village of Vertus. The third release of this wine is big, ripe and concentrated, although perhaps lacking some of the vivacity of the original 2002.

Femme de Champagne 1996

Le Snob ESSENTIAL This is the prestige cuvée of the house, made from the super ripe '96 vintage, which also boasted the highest acidity levels in recent times. This piercingly fresh and citrusy wine took quite a few years to come round but ripe fruit and racy acidity are finally in balance and the result is an exciting, tongue-tingling fizz with an underlying richness emerging.

Billecart-Salmon

40 Rue Carnot, 51160 Mareuil-sur-Ay

Tel: +33 (0)3 26 52 60 22
www.champagne-billecart.fr

François Roland-Billecart is the seventh generation of the family to run this highly regarded house. Over the past few years, the company has increased its annual production to around

1.7 million bottles thanks to access to an extra 80 hectares of vineyard owned by Jean-Jacques Frey, who has a 45 per cent share in the house. While Billecart is particularly admired for its rosé wines, its white vintage wines are arguably the stars, capable of very long ageing and developing deliciously well.

» **Brut Rosé NV**
A gorgeous pale pink, this rosé is positioned very much in the refined, understated, delicately fruity aperitif camp and has many admirers. Initially very fresh, it develops an attractive creaminess if aged for a year or so.

UNIQUE » RARE » LITTLE-KNOWN » ULTIMATE **Snob**

Ungrafted vines At the end of the nineteenth century, phylloxera pest (an aphid that attacks the vine roots) destroyed most of the champagne vineyards. Most vines were replanted on American rootstock to protect them from this disease, but certain areas were unaffected, including three tiny plots (1.4 acres in all) of Pinot Noir – two in the *grand cru* village of Ay and the other in Bouzy. The Bollinger Vieilles Vignes Françaises 2000 is produced from these three plots of ungrafted Pinot Noir. Because of the very low yields, just 3,766 bottles of this Blanc de Noirs style were produced, which cost in the region of £310–£380 a bottle.

>> ### Brut Blanc de Blancs 1998

Le Snob ESSENTIAL It says much about the keeping qualities of the Billecart wines that this cuvée was only starting to reveal its real pedigree and finesse two or three years after its first release. This is partly down to the blend of just three top *grands crus* sites: Cramant for finesse, Avize for its power and Mesnil-sur-Oger for its structure and longevity. As a result it will still develop happily for another decade and may even match the quality and complexity of a recently consumed bottle of the fine vintage 1990. Quince-like aromas highlight the ripeness of the harvest and the palate has a burnished richness likely to turn more chocolately with time.

>> ### Le Clos Saint-Hilaire 1998

Billecart launched this single vineyard wine (100 per cent Pinot Noir that comes from a 1-hectare walled vineyard close to the winery in Mareuil-sur-Ay) with the 1995 vintage released in 2003. This, the third such cuvée first tasted in July 2009, impresses on every level, although the previous '96 cuvée was a hard act to follow in terms of sheer intensity. A golden yellow hue, it shows ripe peachy fruit notes, impressive richness and concentration while retaining a fine, lively, refreshing acidity.

» Regional marques

Regional influence

Although four of these smaller *négociant* houses are located in or on the outskirts of the city of Reims, and Alfred Gratien is in Epernay, most of the others are based in a village or *cru* that plays a central part in the production of their wine and tells us something about them. These houses would consider themselves 'artisan', small-scale producers. The vast majority make fewer than one million bottles a year, some considerably less.

Montagne de Reims

Cattier

6/11, Rue Dom Pérignon,
51500 Chigny les Roses

Tel: + 33 (0)3 26 03 42 11 www.cattier.com

This family-run house based in Chigny-les-Roses, just to the south of Reims, owns 20 hectares of vineyards, much of it rated *premier cru*. Today, Cattier has become better known for its Armand de Brignac brand with its stand-out glitzy packaging in gold, silver and shocking pink respectively for the Brut, Blancs de Blancs and Rosé styles it comes in.

» **Armand de Brignac NV Brut**
This was first launched in 2006 and, like Clos du Moulin, it's also a blend of three harvests, mainly 2005, plus smaller equal amounts of 2003 and 2002.

It has a very low dosage of just 6 g/l so is 'extra brut' in style, but while fresh and lifted thanks to a generous splash of *grand cru* Chardonnay, it is rounded out partly due to the *liqueur de dosage* being aged in oak casks. It has decent length too.

Henriot

81, Rue Coquebert, 51100 Reims

Tel: +33 (0)3 26 89 53 00
www.champagne-henriot.com

The Henriot family has been in Champagne since the sixteenth century. The present head of the company, Joseph Henriot, established Veuve Clicquot's modern reputation before returning to the family business in the nineties. He subsequently spread his family interests further south to Burgundy where he bought and restored the fortunes of Bouchard Père et Fils and William Fèvre. Henriot's champagnes, however, are relatively unknown but are all well made and the vintage wines and deluxe line Cuvée des Enchanteleurs are potential gems that age beautifully.

» Vintage Brut 1996

This is a re-release of a fine vintage that had a magical combination of very ripe fruit and unusually high acidity. This has now developed gloriously, showing lovely concentration and creamy depth, though it is still enlivened by racy acidity, so there is no great hurry to drink it up.

» Cuvée des Enchanteleurs 1995

 This is a champagne to linger over, a wine at, or near, the height of its opulent power. It is to be sipped and savoured on a sunny afternoon in the garden. A blend of 55 per cent Chardonnay and 45 per cent Pinot Noir with a mature toasty nose of heady complexity, the zesty, spicy, exotic fruit gives way to a sumptuous Meursault-like richness on the palate and a long chocolatey finish. You'll find few better examples of the 1995 vintage; most were released years ago and consumed before they reached such a luscious peak.

Krug

5, Rue de Coquebert, 51100 Reims

Tel: +33 (0)3 26 84 44 20 www.krug.com

Olivier Krug is the sixth generation of the Krug family to head up this famous house. Producer of the most exclusive and highest priced wines in the appellation, Krug champagnes are renowned for their longevity and rich, vinous style. Unlike any other house in Champagne, all the wines fit within the prestige cuvée sector and all retail for over £100 a bottle – some considerably more.

» Krug Grande Cuvée

The Krug Grande Cuvée is a multi-vintage blend, where even the youngest component gets at least five years ageing on its yeast lees and some reserve elements are 20 years old. The style is distinctively rich and developed with secondary aromas of brioche, vanilla, mocha, plus smoky, spicy notes coming partly from fermentation in small oak casks and long ageing. Complexity is added by the significant amount (sometimes as high as 50 per cent) of reserve wine in the blend.

>> Vintage 1996

One of the greatest Krug vintage wines ever made, it's still possible to get hold of this impressive, super-charged, super-concentrated champagne, which shows off all the best facets of this potentially great vintage – amazing vitality borne of very high acidity and great richness from one of the ripest harvests on record. The finish is powerful, penetratingly vivid and very long indeed in the mouth.

>> Krug Clos du Mesnil 1996

Le Snob ESSENTIAL This is a single-vineyard wine from a 1.87 hectare vineyard, in Le Mesnil-sur-Oger, and is 100 per cent Chardonnay. With a year like 1996, where the Krug vintage is so impressive in every way, it is very hard to imagine that Clos du Mesnil could surpass it but tasted side by side that is precisely what it does manage. The palate intensity is startling, the texture silken. Notes of ripe exotic fruit and lime are cut with mouth-watering acidity before a creamy richness fills the mouth and leads to a long, powerful finish. It has more to reveal over the next decade or so.

>> Clos d'Ambonnay 1996

As we have seen, 1996 was a very particular year in Champagne, generally producing wines with intense acidity and high ripeness levels. Both show up in the Krug, which at first appears rich, ripe and evolved with developed toasty, bready aromas. On the palate however it is still intensely fresh and citrusy, and has a very long life ahead – a couple of decades or more. The price has actually dropped a little since the original lauch to between £1,200 and £1,400 a bottle.

Champagne Marguet Père & Fils

1, Place Barancourt, 51150 Ambonnay

Tel: +33 (0)3 26 53 78 61
www.champagne-marguet.fr

Benoit Marguet is a fifth-generation vine grower. He has set out in a new direction: converting to organic farming wherever possible, ploughing by horse, using 90 per cent oak fermentation and seeking to make wines with a strong individual character.

UNIQUE » RARE » LITTLE-KNOWN » ULTIMATE Snob

Tiny vineyards The Clos d'Ambonnay is produced from a tiny 0.685 hectares site right next to the village of Ambonnay, a single vineyard, single varietal (Pinot Noir) Champagne from Krug. For the first vintage of 1995, 3,000 bottles were made, and when they went on sale in 2007, the asking price was around £2,100.

Blanc de Noirs Brut NV

This 2006/2007 blend is a 75 per cent Pinot Noir and 25 per cent Pinot Meunier Blanc de Noirs. It is attractively fruited with big flavours, mineral notes, a biscuity texture and good mouthfeel; an expressive and impressive wine with lots of life and energy.

Grand Cru Rosé Brut NV

There is just Ambonnay and Bouzy fruit (70 per cent Chardonnay and 30 per cent Pinot Noir) in this pretty, pale pink champagne with orange highlights; the colour comes from a 12 per cent portion vinified as red wine, plus 1 per cent from *saignée*. Made in a clean, fresh lifted style – thanks partly to a portion of Cramant and Le Mesni-sur-Oger Chardonnay – there is also a dense black fruit component.

Grand Cru Brut Millésimé 2002

This is a blend of 70 per cent Chardonnay and 30 per cent Pinot Noir made entirely from *grands crus* in the Montagne de Reims and Côte des Blancs. With rich, plump, ripe peachy fruit and a velvety soft texture, this also has some spiciness and mineral intensity.

Bruno Paillard

Avenue de Champagne, 51100 Reims

Tel: +33 (0)3 26 36 20 22
www.champagnebrunopaillard.com

This is a thoroughly modern house: the 'cellars' are all above ground in a large, temperature-controlled warehouse, using the latest technology. Bruno Paillard, who established his 'new house' at the age of 27 in 1981, quickly gained a reputation for the quality of his own wines. Since 1985, Paillard's wines have shown the date of disgorgement, an enlightened policy that more and more quality producers are following today.

» Brut Première Cuvée NV

An elegant, fresh, citrus-tinged style (although only one-third Chardonnay) that boasts an underlying depth and richness thanks to good use of reserve wines, which make up to between 20 and 50 per cent of the blend. This wine can age impressively, going buttery rich with spicy gingerbread notes, as a tasting of this wine (based on the 1995 harvest with a dozen years post-disgorgement age) showed recently.

» Rosé Première Cuvée NV

A lovely, delicate, pale onion skin colour, this lightly fruity rosé has real class and finesse, something to savour on a warm summer's evening al fresco or great for a special aperitif. It is served in some of the best hotel bars in Paris including Le Meurice.

» Grande Cuvée Nec Plus Ultra 1995

This prestige line is given the extra ageing a *grand cru* luxury cuvée deserves before release but in today's climate rarely gets. It is sourced from seven *grands crus* and is barrel-fermented, with two years post-disgorgement rest before release and a low dosage of just 4 g/l. Waxy mouth texture, toastiness and a hint of honey come out as it opens in the glass.

» Brut Millésimé 1996 Blanc de Blancs

Le Snob ESSENTIAL Few houses manage to keep back vintage releases, even when years like 1996 demand it, but this beauty from Paillard, which has the concentration and structure to deserve such

» Single vineyard vs blends

Blending good champagne is about picking the best
still wines and combining those that work together.
When blending a top wine, a producer is looking for
complexity but not necessarily power. And that's
where the style of single vineyard and blended wines
are different. Complexity in a blend comes from
having different component parts but a single
vineyard wine has to come from an exceptional plot
of land, one that has been found to produce
something special. For example, when my great
uncle Pierre Philipponnat bought Clos des Goisses
in 1935 he immediately knew he'd make a single
vineyard wine from this site.

These champagnes are more about individuality
and power, they're more wine-like. We suggest
decanting Clos des Goisses and not serving it too
cool, about 12°C, to reveal these facets.

treatment, only came on to the market in 2010. All *grand cru*, the whole batch disgorged in November 2007, this is still very young, quite tight, very fresh with intense citrus spice like an ice cold shower to the mouth but with impressive concentration.

Vallée de la Marne

Ayala

Château d'Aÿ, 2, Boulevard du Nord, 51160 Aÿ

Tel: +33 (0)3 26 55 15 44
www.champagne-ayala.fr

This previously little-known house was purchased by the Bollinger group in 2005 and since the takeover MD Hervé Augustin has set out to raise its profile and draw attention to its well-made wines. He has done this partly by lowering dosage levels across the range, in line with the modern trend among small go-ahead producers, but he has also gone a step further by introducing completely non-dosé versions of three of the regular cuvées: Brut Majeur non-vintage and Brut Majeur Rosé non-vintage wines and prestige line Perle d'Ayala. Augustin also gives the date of disgorgement on the back labels.

» **Ayala Zéro Dosage NV**
While some companies put together a different blend for their low or no dosage champagnes, what's particularly interesting about Ayala is that they use the same blend as the standard Brut Majeur NV (which itself has only a low dosage of 8.5 g/l) but no

sugar is added at the point of disgorgement. Impressively, the resulting wine is not overly austere. It has good aromatics and shows some finesse and depth thanks to the quality of the *crus* used and the proportion of reserve wine (which is around 20 per cent). In fact there's a mineral quality that appears to give it more palate texture.

» Perle d'Ayala 2002

Le Snob ESSENTIAL This top-of-the-range wine is made by blending 20 per cent Pinot Noir from Aÿ with the Blanc de Blancs vintage cuvée that Ayala produces. This was a dazzling wine itself in 2002, emanating from three *grands crus* Blanc de Blancs vineyards, and its high-quality pedigree shows in classy, elegant wine, still quite steely in its relative youth after eight years ageing. Fresh and zesty with some grapefruit notes, it's taut and intense but will open with more time.

067

Deutz

16, Rue Jeanson, 51160 Aÿ

Tel: +33 (0)3 26 56 94 00
www.champagne-deutz.com

This traditional house, built its reputation under the management of five generations of the Lallier-Deutz family prior to a friendly takeover by like-minded quality producer Louis Roederer back in 1993. Since then, with increased investment its fine range of champagnes has hit new heights of excellence. The understated wines mainly available in the top end of the restaurant trade are well worth seeking out.

>> ## Deutz Brut Classic NV

Le Snob ESSENTIAL This wine is a fine blueprint for the qualities needed in a top class non-vintage Champagne. Initially deliciously fresh, it has enough age on release to have developed genuine depth of texture and flavour. As well as citrus highlights in this lively sherbetty fizz, there are ripe peachy fruit flavours and a fine-grained creamy texture plus yeasty, savoury notes of maturity.

>> ## Brut Vintage Rosé 2005

Antique pink in colour, with hints of orange, this satisfyingly ample rosé is wholly made from top-quality Pinot Noir. The colour and some of the depth results from the 10 per cent that has been vinified as red wine, which comes from Deutz top vineyard parcels on the south-facing slopes above the village of Aÿ. This gives it the structure and power to successfully match the fattiness of roast duck or rack of lamb.

>> ## Deutz Blanc de Blancs 2004

This is always one of the most dazzling wines in the range with a sherbetty zip that dances lightly across the tongue underpinned by a biscuity palate texture; an all-Chardonnay style of real finesse.

Gosset

69, Rue Jules Blondeau, 51160 Aÿ

Tel: +33 (0)3 26 56 99 56
www.champagne-gosset.com

Gosset, based in the *grand cru* village of Aÿ, is the oldest wine house in Champagne, established in 1584. Originally it made mostly table wine as Aÿ, along with Beaune, was the main source of red wine for the French court in the sixteenth century. Today it produces full-bodied and richly aromatic champagnes that age particularly well and, because of their affinity with food, are often to be found on good restaurant wine lists.

›› Gosset Grand Rosé Brut NV

An attractive salmon pink, the wine is lifted by a large slug of Chardonnay in the blend (56 per cent) while depth comes from red wine sourced from *grands crus* villages Ambonnay and Bouzy. It has lovely fruit and mouthfeel with a creamy texture but also some zip; a delightful drink.

›› Gosset Grande Réserve NV Brut

Le Snob ESSENTIAL A three-vintage blend (currently 2002, 2003 and 2005) that is aged for five years, Grande Réserve is mostly Chardonnay (43 per cent) and Pinot Noir (42 per cent) with a dash of Pinot Meunier in the mix to add fruity aromas. It's one of the best non-vintage champagnes on the market, with developed aromas of brioche, vanilla and ripe stone fruit. Its soft and silky, rich palate seduces and it has an interesting spicy, savoury element with a hint of lightly roasted coffee on the finish.

Gosset Grand Millésimé 2000

This is made in different vintages to Celebris (see below), but while less expensive it can be very expressive. The blend is a mix of Chardonnay and Pinot Noir that's already quite developed, with rich, warm, spicy notes leading to hints of leather and smoke. It's a big, powerful, characterful champagne, that is not for the faint-hearted.

Celebris Vintage 1998 Extra Brut

The Celebris trio are all serious wines: vintaged, low dosage and with a long ageing potential. Although made in the classic Gosset style and still youthful, this cuvée has an intensity of flavour and already shows quite a bit of complexity.

Alfred Gratien

30, Rue Maurice Cerveaux, 51201 Epernay

Tel: + 33 (0)3 26 54 38 20 www.alfredgratien.com

This very traditional producer still ferments all of its champagne in small oak casks and makes very expressive, long-lived wines. Although the brand is now owned by a German Sekt producer, Henkell & Co., the production methods haven't changed, and Chef de Cave Jean-Paul Jaegar recently passed the baton to his son Nicolas.

Brut NV

Le Snob ESSENTIAL This regularly gets four years ageing in the Gratien cellars before release, rather than the more normal two to three that most non-vintage cuvées receive. A pale lemon colour, it's quite ripe and rich on the nose, very fresh and lively initially with good intensity of flavour. This is a top-class fizz that puts many bigger names to shame.

>> **Brut Vintage 1999**
Made from two-thirds Chardonnay, around a quarter Pinot Noir and 10 per cent Pinot Meunier, this is a full-bodied style with great aromatics and length. Already showing some of its hallmark toastiness but could comfortably age another five years or more. It still needs time to come out of its shell.

>> **Cuvée Paradis NV**
Although it doesn't carry a vintage on the label, this prestige cuvée is actually all produced from the 2005 harvest, so it has over five years bottle age. The blend majors on Chardonnay (65 per cent) with similar

Date of disgorgement

There is a growing movement in Champagne for producers of all types, particularly growers and smaller specialist houses, to put more information on their bottles, such as the exact blend, the harvest base of non vontage cuvées, the portion of reserve wine, dosage levels, and the date of disgorgement. For consumers, knowing the date of disgorgement allows them to drink the wines when they are young and fresh within a few months of the disgorgement, or choose to age them longer in their own cellars 'on the cork', perhaps several years until they have developed further richness and aromatic complexity.

amounts of Pinots Noir and Meunier. Like the other Gratien wines, it doesn't undergo malolatic fermentation (see page 18) which amplifies the freshness. There are lemon citrus aromas initially with a hint of vanilla, some spiciness and a honeyed note on the finish.

Jacquesson

68, Rue du Colonel Fabien, 51530 Dizy

Tel: + 33 (0)3 26 55 68 11
www.champagnejacquesson.com

This top-class small producer is run by brothers Jean-Hervé and Laurent Chiquet, who have established an enviable reputation for the quality of the Jacquesson wines and all aspects of their operation. The great care they take starts in the vineyard where they employ traditional methods of viticulture, farming largely organically, and eschew the use of herbicides. Only the cuvée is used and vinification takes place in large oak *foudres*. Uniquely their non-vintage Champagne is not a consistent style but a one-off that changes each year to produce the best possible blend they can make from any individual harvest.

» Jacquesson Cuvée 734

Lemon-yellow with golden highlights, it has a citrusy streak of acidity, an attractive nutty intensity and quite a silky, creamy palate. Already gathering richness, this particular cuvée is noticeably less austere at this stage than some of its predecessors were, though still well short of its peak. These wines mature in much the same as vintage champagne, gathering complexity as they age.

>> **Jacquesson 2002 Vintage**

Le Snob ESSENTIAL The last vintage blend made by this house is a wine to seek out and savour. Opulent and rich on the nose with developed secondary, spicy, yeasty notes this has a balancing acidity, fine palate texture and expressive minerality. It finishes on a glorious note that seems to last for an eternity. Superb

Alain Thienot

14, Rue des Moissons, 51100 Reims

Tel: +33 (0)3 26 77 50 10 www.thienot.com

This is a true family business, with Alain Thiénot taking more of a back seat while his son Stanislas and daughter Garance increasingly run things. They have invested substantially in a new state-of-the-art winery, which was only completed in 2003. The estate was built up by Alain, based on vineyards in the *grands crus* of Le Mesnil-sur-Oger and Aÿ, and has grown to 27 hectares, half of which are *premier* and *grand cru*. The wines are classical and elegant.

>> **Thiénot Brut Rosé NV**

Le Snob ESSENTIAL At a tasting of non-vintage rosé champagnes, this stood out from the crowd. Made from 45 per cent Chardonnay, 28 per cent Pinot Noir, 20 per cent Pinot Meunier, and the crucial addition of 7 per cent red wine from one of the oldest vineyards in Aÿ, it is a class act with attractive raspberry fruit and a nice refreshing grip of acidity.

» **Thiénot Brut NV**

A high proportion of Chardonnay helps give this cuvée delicious freshness and finesse. It boasts good concentration and depth, too, partly thanks to a decent proportion of reserve wine. It is very enjoyable and a step up in quality from many more lofty names.

Joseph Perrier

69, Avenue de Paris,
51016 Châlons-en-Champagne

Tel: +33 (0)3 26 68 29 51 www.josephperrier.com

This is the only house making champagne in the agreeable town of Châlon-en-Champagne, several miles east of the main Marne Valley vineyards. Joseph Perrier actually owns vines in the heart of the appellation while it buys in Chardonnay from Avize and Le Mesnil-sur-Oger in the Côte des Blancs. Run by the highly charismatic and hospitable Jean-Claude Fourmon, whose family are deeply rooted in the region, this fine house produces wines of great charm and serious vintage cuvées.

» **Blanc de Blancs Vintage 2002**

Le Snob ESSENTIAL A new cuvée of very high quality from this great vintage, where the Chardonnay was the pick of the crop, that's a step up in concentration and intensity from the already good non-vintage style. There is plenty of finesse, lovely richness and impressive length, as you might expect from something sourced from top vineyards in Le Mesnil-sur-Oger, Avize and Cumières.

» Cuvée Josephine 2002

There was a jump of four years from the rich and forward 1998 vintage to the top-class 2002 for this prestige style is a blend of 56 per cent Chardonnay and 44 per cent Pinot Noir, all sourced from *premiers* and *grands crus* vineyards. Currently it's taut and fresh with bright, vivid fruit leading to a rich palate that is dominated by the ripe Chardonnay of this expressive vintage, and a touch of spice on the finish. If true to form, it will go deliciously toasty with age. There is no hurry to drink it up.

» Brut Rosé Vintage 2002

A partner for the Blanc de Blancs vintage, also new and from the quality 2002 harvest. Classy, fruity and intense, it is a satin-textured rosé that's mainly Pinot Noir, freshened with a dash of Chardonnay and made by the addition of 12 per cent red wine from Cumières. It has a spicy, toasty character on the finish. Because Joseph Perrier is not as widely renowned as the quality of its wines deserve, it's also priced very attractively at a similar level to some top-rated non-vintage rosés.

In the details

The importance of using
reserve wine in blends

» Reserve wine

Nearly all champagne houses that produce non-
vintage champagne use reserve wines in their blends
– it is entirely legal to make non-vintage champagne
all from one harvest but is not usual. Originally reserve
wines were used to bring uniformity of style and taste
to non-vintage champagne. This is particularly true
of the large-volume international brands, as they like
to preserve a recognisable taste profile however
much the base harvest changes from year to year.

As well as promoting regularity of style, among
quality-minded producers reserve wine is also
increasingly employed to add nuances of flavour,
complexity and finesse, and to give character and
distinctiveness. It may be overstating the case to
claim that non-vintage champagnes with a large
proportion of reserve wines in them are necessarily
better, but it's certainly true to say that, with higher
proportions of reserve wine, you are likely to find
greater complexity and more interesting wine.

Philipponnat

13, Rue du Pont, 51160 Mareuil-sur-Aÿ

Tel: +33 (0)3 26 56 93 01 www.philipponnat.com

The quality across the whole Pinot Noir-dominated range at Philipponnat has improved impressively over the past five years under Charles Philipponnat's skilful management, particularly the non-vintage Royale Réserve. Better use is being made of the 20 hectares of vines that the company owns in some of the best *crus* on the southern slopes of the Montagne de Reims. The jewel in its crown remains Clos des Goisses, a steep 5.5-hectare, south-facing vineyard on pure chalky soils, which produces some of the ripest and richest wine in the whole of Champagne.

» Royale Réserve Brut NV

Elegant, biscuity with a creamy richness and good texture in the mouth, this has become one of the best non-vintage champagnes in the appellation. Complexity is added by quite a high portion of reserve wine and the fact that these reserves from previous harvests are now kept in oak barrels.

» Cuvée 1522 Millésime 2000

This wine, a rich and pure 60/40 Pinot Noir-Chardonnay blend, commemorates the first historical record of the Philipponnat family in the village of Mareuil-sur-Aÿ. Already quite rich, toasty with generosity of flavour and aroma, this vintage has elegance too, but hasn't yet reached its peak.

Clos des Goisses 1998

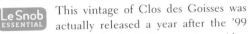 This vintage of Clos des Goisses was actually released a year after the '99 vintage, because, as Charles Philipponnat says, it's a massive, deeply structured wine of great intensity and it needed more time for its diverse elements to integrate better. He says it has the potential to age for decades not just a few more years and there is evidence in the bottle – great structure and concentration – to support this viewpoint.

Côte des Bar

Drappier

Rue des Vignes, Urville, 10200 Urville

Tel: + 33 (0)3 25 27 40 15
www.champagne-drappier.com

Michel Drappier makes a fine selection of mostly Pinot Noir-based, characterful, expressive wines, some of which hint at the close physical proximity of Burgundy. He's even devised a special decanter to help intensify the powerful vinous aromas. The range includes a fine, mineral all-Pinot Noir Brut Nature champagne, mainly sold in French restaurants, plus an innovative four varietal Blanc de Blancs blend (Cuvée Quattuor), of Chardonnay, Pinot Blanc and rarities Arbane and Petit Meslier.

Val des Demoiselles Brut Rosé NV

This wine looks more like a light Burgundian red, with ripe, delicious Pinot Noir fruit dominating the palate. It's made by the *saignée* method. The resulting concentration of red fruit is so strong that Michel Drappier actually lightens it slightly by the addition of a little Pinot Noir vinified as white wine, but the final colour of the wine varies depending on which harvest it is based. This is one of the very best non-vintage rosés around and not at all expensive.

» Cuvée Millésimé Exception 2002

The 2002 vintage in champagne is arguably the most consistently good year for over a decade. Nearly all the wines have looked attractive at release while also showing good ageing potential. This Drappier vintage is another fine example of the genre, at once ample, forward, rich and beautifully balanced. While it's highly enjoyable now, with a few years of extra cellaring, it will develop greater complexity.

» Grande Sendrée Vintage 2002

Le Snob ESSENTIAL Produced from a steep south-facing site in Urville, this blend of 45 per cent Chardonnay and 55 per cent Pinot Noir is the prestige cuvée of the house and the star of the range. Silky textured, rich, but beautifully balanced it has more than of whiff of Burgundy about it, as well as floral notes, aromas of dried flowers and hints of mandarin, soft spices and sweet honey.

» Brut Nature

This non-dosé, 100 per cent Pinot Noir champagne was first launched in 1999. Clean fresh, with a salty, mineral, almost iodine note, it makes a fine palate-cleansing aperitif or excellent accompaniment to a plate of oysters.

Côte des Blancs

Champagne Veuve Fourny et Fils

12-5, Rue du Mesnil, 51130 Vertus

Tel: +33(0)3 26 52 16 30
www.champagne-veuve-fourny.com

Emmanuel and Charles-Henry Fourny run this family business scrupulously – and with great attention to detail. Their reputation for producing pure, refined, long-lived, low and zero-dosage wines is definitely in the ascendance. They farm some 15 hectares of vineyards with 40 separate parcels of land, all located within the highly rated *premier cru* of Vertus, mostly planted with Chardonnay on three different soil types.

» Cuvée 'R' Extra Brut NV

Le Snob ESSENTIAL Named after their father, Roger Fourny, this superb wine is made with a majority of Chardonnay and a *soupçon* of Pinot Noir. It comes from organically grown vines that are an average age of 39 years old and produce a concentrated, richly aromatic juice. It is made from a high-quality base of 2002 and 2004, all vinified in small oak casks. Elegant, energetic, poised, initially there are aromas of white flower and fresh citrus fruits. On the palate there is a distinct saline note and savoury, complex, smoky, yeasty Marmite flavours evolve in the glass while a streak of mineral purity is maintained in the long, rich finish.

>> **Clos des Faubourgs de Notre Dame 1999**
Emanating from a tiny walled single-vineyard plot of about half an acre, replanted in 1951, this all-Chardonnay cuvée has more colour and intensity, some fatness in the mouth, plus a marked chalky minerality. A long-lived classy fizz that will develop more creaminess as it ages, only a few hundred bottles are made each vintage.

Salon

5-7 Rue de la Brèche d'Oger,
51190 Le Mesnil-sur-Oger

Tel: +33 33 (0)3 26 57 51 65
www.salondelamotte.com

These two houses owned by the Laurent-Perrier group share premises in Le Mesnil-sur-Oger but Salon is unusual in producing just one cuvée, all from Le Mesnil fruit, and not every harvest. Its fine, extremely long-lived Blanc de Blancs style is always vintaged and only made in the best years. The Delamotte cuvées benefit as they take the Le Mesnil fruit in the many years that Salon is not made.

>> **Salon 1997**
In their youth (which may last a dozen years or more) these wines are often unapproachably steely and quite impenetrable, even unattractive. They really need time to show complexity in addition to the core of pure, saline elegance.

» Growers

Growing individuality

Only about half of the growers that make and sell champagne under their own label export it to markets outside France and between them they account for no more than 5 per cent of total champagne exports. Quite a chunk of this is very basic fizz, but there is a growing band of artisan producers that make small volumes of individual and characterful wine that reflects the specific *terroir* – often just one *cru* or village in the region – on which it is produced. Interest in these champagnes is developing rapidly, partly in reaction to the uniformity and dullness of some of the big brands. This is where to find much of the current vinous excitement in the region, while the wines offer a particularly good quality-to-price ratio.

West and south-west of Reims

Chartogne-Taillet

37, Grand-Rue, 51220 Merfy

Tel: +33 (0)3 26 03 10 17
http://chartogne-taillet.typepad.fr

This quality grower-producer, based in the sleepy village of Merfy, is now run by Alexandre Chartogne-Taillet who took over from his parents in 2006. While its reputation for its wines was already established, he has brought in new ideas both about how they farm (ending the use of herbicides and pesticides, ploughing between the vines by horse) and how the wines are made, such as lowering sulphur and dosage levels and introducing some oak.

>> Millésimé 2002 Brut

This poised 50/50 Pinot Noir-Chardonnay blend from the exceptional 2002 harvest is satisfyingly Pinot-rich with meaty, savoury notes, a yeasty, chewy palate texture plus a hint of minerality and spiciness. The dosage is low, at 7 g/l.

>> Cuvée Sainte Anne Brut NV

This wine is 60 per cent Chardonnay, 40 per cent Pinot Noir blend, and is based on the 2006 harvest with 20 per cent reserve wine from 2005 and 2004. Disgorged in November 2009, it's unfiltered and unfined, and the dosage is low enough (at 4.5 g/l) to make it an 'extra brut' style, which helps preserve good freshness and vivacity. With notes of freshly baked pastries, it also has an attractive ripe peach fruit element and good length.

>> Cuvée Fiacre 'Tête de Cuvée'

Fiacre is their prestige cuvée and, although unvintaged on the label, actually comes from a single harvest, 2002 in this case. Made from a 60 per cent Chardonnay, 40 per cent Pinot Noir blend this is an ample, complex and expressive wine with impressive concentration and a long finish.

Jérôme Prévost

2, Rue Petite Montagne, 51390 Gueux

Tel: +33 (0)3 26 03 48 60

Jérôme Prévost's tiny production of some 13,000 bottles of oak-fermented, Pinot Meunier-based champagne are much sought after. He makes one main wine, plus a tiny production of rosé, from 2 hectares of bio-dynamically farmed 40-year-old Pinot Meunier, though he also has an additional 0.2 hectares plot planted with young vines of other varieties. As well as fermenting in oak, the wines are all made with natural yeasts, without fining or filtering and using as little sulphur as possible. No dosage is added on disgorgement.

» La Closerie Les Béguines Brut Nature

Le Snob ESSENTIAL This wine, which is made entirely from the 2006 harvest with no reserve wine as usual, accounts for the majority of production. Powerful, lively, intensely expressive, it's outside most peoples' experience of champagne. It is very vinous, with developed, yeasty smoky aromas that follow through in the rich palate and a long and complex finish.

Champagne Maillart

5, Rue de Villers aux Noeuds, 51500 Ecueil

Tel: + 33(0)3 26 49 77 89
www.champagne-maillart.fr

Nicolas Maillart is another 'young' winemaker who has revolutionised the way he makes wine. He now widely uses oak fermentation, experimenting with locally produced barrels, has generally reduced dosage levels, and has increased the reserve wine element in his blends.

» Maillart Brut Rosé Grand Cru NV (Bouzy)

This is a blend of 70 per cent Pinot Noir and 30 per cent Chardonnay, with an attractive salmon-pink colour extracted by maceration from the skins of the black grapes. There is a portion of oak-fermented wine in the blend to add complexity plus a light dosage of 6 g/l to keep the style fresh and elegant. With notes of ripe fruits and a vanilla element coming partly from the oak, the powerful Bouzy fruit is evident.

» Les Franc de Pieds 2003 Extra Brut Premier Cru

Le Snob ESSENTIAL Only made in the best vintages, this wine comes from a south-facing, small 'ungrafted' Pinot Noir vineyard in Ecueil, planted in 1973. It's fermented and aged in oak vats with *batonnage* (lees stirring) while the malolactic fermentation is blocked to help preserve freshness. It's bottled unfiltered with virtually no dosage (just 2 g/l). Golden hued with intense ripe fruit aromas, hints of almond and a rich caramel note, it's a pure and expressive *terroir*-driven wine.

» Premier Cru Brut NV Platine

This assemblage of 80 per cent Pinot Noir and 20 per cent Chardonnay has between 30 and 40 per cent reserve wine (depending on the harvest) that's been aged in oak in the blend and this helps allow a relatively low dosage of 7 g/l. With a fine mousse of persistent small bubbles, it's full of life with a taut, clean, fresh lifted style, some grapefruit citrus notes, good intensity and a long clean finish.

Bérèche et Fils

Le Craon de Ludes, 51500 Ludes

Tel: +33 (0)3 26 61 13 28
www.champagne-bereche-et-fils.com

The Bérèche family has 9.3 hectares of vineyard in six different *crus*, mostly in what is known as the Petit Montagne de Reims. They treat their soils with respect, eschewing chemical treatments, using horses to plough between vines and gradually increasing the proportion they farm bio-dynamically. Yields are generally kept much lower than the average in Champagne with an annual production of around 85,000 bottles. They take a non-interventional approach to winemaking using natural yeasts for the initial ferments which partly take place in oak, without any malolactic fermentation or filtering, and low dosage levels.

» Extra Brut Réserve NV

The purity of flavours in the Bérèche wines is particularly noticeable in this extra brut style that has just a 2 g/l dosage, giving a nicely defined mineral touch, fine mouth texture with dried fruit notes and a hint of bitterness on the finish. Like the excellent straight-brut style this is also a three-way blend of Chardonnay, Pinot Meunier and Pinot Noir, which is 15 per cent oak fermented with 30 per cent reserve wine from the two previous harvests, but it gets a year's extra ageing before release.

>> **Reflet d'Antan**

The most expensive Bérèche wine is matured in barrels for nearly a year following some 18 months ageing on fine lees in tanks and has been produced since 1985 under their version of the 'solera system' (see page 90). So the current blend on the market has a small element of reserve wine that dates back 25 years. With a harvest base of 2004, although extra brut in style (6 g/l dosage), this wine – and it is more wine than champagne – is full-bodied, rich, complex and evolved, with pronounced yeasty aromas and a very creamy palate plus a savoury note on the finish.

Dehours & Fils

2, Rue de la Chapelle, 51700 Cerseuil

Tel: +33 (0)3 26 52 71 75
www.champagne-dehours.fr

Fourth-generation independent grower, Jérôme Dehours, along with his brother-in-law Jean-Marc Laisne, produces a fine range of champagnes from their numerous parcels of vines split between Mareuil-le-Port, Oeuilly and Troissy. Jérôme uses a *perpétuelle réserve* first set up in 1998 for his five white non-vintage blends with Trio 'S' Brut, a three-varietal blend that comes entirely from this 'solera' system. He also makes two single-vineyard, vintage

» The solera system

Some champagne wine reserves are run in a way
that's similar to the solera system used in the
production of sherry. At its simplest this might
involve combining the non-vintage cuvée blend with
a certain amount (10 to 20 per cent) of the previous
year's non-vintage release, which is kept back for this
purpose. This adds nuances of complexity to the new
cuvée and each succeeding year this base wine will
gradually contain more and older component parts.
Bruno Paillard's and Philipponnat's main non-
vintage cuvées both employ such a system.

Other producers have taken the idea a stage further
and developed what is being called a *réserve
perpétuelle*, involving a number of barrels. For each
non-vintage cuvée produced, a certain amount of
reserve wine (perhaps a third of the blend) is taken
from the last barrel and combined with the new
harvest. A portion of this new non-vintage blend is
used each year to top up the first barrel in the 'solera'.

champagnes, one a Blanc de Noirs the other a three-way blend from two parcels of land in Mareuil-le-Port.

» La Côte en Bosses 2004 Mareuil-le-Port Extra Brut

This is the sort of wine that is drawing attention to a small band of quality champagne growers pushing the boundaries. An extraordinary blend of all three main grape varieties from old vines fermented in small oak *barriques*, just 2,681 bottles were produced in 2004, and they were disgorged on 7 Jan 2010 in an extra brut style with just 4 g/l dosage. This is a complex, developed wine of real palate weight and intensity that remains lively and vigorous.

» Maisoncelle 2004 Mareuil-le-Port Extra Brut

This wine comes from a very small parcel of old vines of Pinot Noir plus a minute amount of un-grafted Meunier. Just 3,047 bottles were made in 2004. It was disgorged in 2010 with a dosage of just 3 g/l. Fresh and even citrusy initially, this has a noticeable saline, mineral quality and a savoury intensity that makes it stand out from the crowd.

Montagne de Reims

Vilmart & Cie

5, Rue des Gravières, 51500 Rilly-la-Montagne

Tel: +33 (0)3 26 03 40 01
www.champagnevilmart.fr

In the early 1990s, Vilmart was one of the first grower producers to establish a reputation for its wines outside France, which now command quite serious prices. Based in the pretty and quiet backwater of Rilly-la-Montagne on the northern slopes of the Montagne de Reims, and run by Laurent Champs, they own 11 hectares of *premiers crus* vineyards mostly planted with Chardonnay (60 per cent) and Pinot Noir (37 per cent) plus just 3 per cent Meunier, which are farmed largely organically.

» Grand Cellier Brut NV

While Grand Reserve is 70 per cent Pinot Noir, the Chardonnay-dominant (70 per cent) Grand Cellier, which is aged a year longer, is more expressive. A lifted, energetic fizz with a pronounced spiciness, it also has a developed, quite exotic, fruit richness and shows impressive concentration.

» Coeur de Cuvée 2000

Le Snob ESSENTIAL This wine is 80 per cent Chardonnay and 20 per cent Pinot Noir, made and aged in new and one-year-old barriques, though the oak seems restrained. It comes from the two best Vilmart vineyards plus the oldest vines, and this shows in greater freshness, more finesse and a noticeably long finish though it will develop more with extra ageing.

Paul Déthune

2, Rue du Moulin, 51150 Ambonnay

Tel: + 33 (0)3 26 57 01 88
www.champagne-dethune.com

Pierre and Sophie Déthune produce an attractive range of wines from the seven hectare vineyard they farm sustainably. While stainless steel fermentation has become the norm in Champagne, many new generation growers are returning to either total or partial oak fermenting and ageing with good results. The Déthune wines are a good example of this and their wines beautifully express the ampleness and richness of Ambonnay fruit.

094

» Grand Cru Blancs de Noirs

Although this isn't declared as a vintage, it's all from the 2006 harvest and is both fermented and aged in used oak barrels. Rich and rounded, but not at all heavy, it shows an attractive honeyed, beeswax note along with a nice depth of red berry fruit.

» Brut Prestige

This is a 50/50 blend of Chardonnay and Pinot Noir, made from a harvest base of 2002 with 25 per cent reserve wines. The nose is developed with aromas of toasted bread and dried fruit, while the palate texture is seductively soft and creamy thanks to the Chardonnay, with notes of vanilla and a spicy, gingerbread element. Ambonnay Chardonnay is called 'Pinote' because it gives this lush, plump fruit and takes on some characteristics of Pinot Noir.

Rodez

4, Rue de Isse, 51150 Ambonnay

Tel: +33 (0)3 26 57 04 93
www.champagne-rodez.fr

After working with other vignerons, Eric Rodez
returned to the family domain in 1982 and set about
introducing changes based on his experiences. His
6.5 hectares of vineyard in the *grand cru* of
Ambonnay are farmed with minimal chemical
treatments. Planted with 55 per cent Pinot Noir and 45
per cent Chardonnay, all 35 parcels are vinified
separately, giving a wide range of blending options.

» **Rodez Cuvée des Crayères Brut NV**
This is a six-harvest blend, mostly 2004, but also
2003 and 2002, with additional small splashes of

Crémant style

To get champagne, or any sparkling wine, to re-
ferment for a second time in the bottle (to create
bubbles) a certain amount of yeast, yeast nutrients
and sugar are added to the final blend of still wine.
The amount of sugar depends on the degree of
effervescence required. Most champagne is fully
mousseux, that is to say a sparkling wine with a
pressure of 5 to 6 atmospheres. There are however
a few champagnes deliberately made in a *crémant*
style (such as Mumm de Cramant) at a slightly
lower pressure (3.6 atmospheres) and these tend to
taste slightly softer, creamier and are less fizzy.

2001, 2000 and 1999 (with equal parts Chardonnay and Pinot Noir). It has an attractive, developed style with floral notes and some honeyed richness.

›› Rodez 2000 Millésimé

A 50/50 Pinot Noir-Chardonnay blend, with 80 per cent vinified in oak, this has a lovely rich golden colour and is surprisingly fresh with a clean bright finish, while the well-integrated oak just plays a supporting role.

›› Rodez Grand Vintages

This is a complex blend of diminishing portions of the best recent vintages, seven in this case (2000, 1999, 1998, 1996, 1995, 1993, 1992) and it's all vinified in oak. A rich, vinous style, it has a lovely silky texture but retains a decent freshness too.

Roger Brun

10, Rue St Vincent, 51160 Aÿ

Tel: +33 (0)3 26 55 45 50
www.champagne-roger-brun.com

Located in the centre of an important *grand cru* village, this fine grower-producer is now run by the friendly and charismatic Philippe Brun, who operates one of the main presses in Aÿ. Philippe makes an excellent range of aromatic, characterful champagnes, using the family vineyards, which are mainly located in Aÿ.

›› Aÿ Grand Cru Brut NV

A Blanc de Noirs all from the *grand cru* of Aÿ, this is a wine of structure and finesse with a freshness and purity of fruit in its youth that shows its pedigree and encourages the extra cellaring it will benefit from, developing more richness and complexity over time.

>> **Cuvée des Sires 99/00**

This is one of Brun's top cuvées, a blend of Aÿ Pinot Noir (around 70 per cent) and Chardonnay from some of his best plots of vineyard. It is vinified in old oak barrels and has a low dosage of 8 g/l. On first release (typically after at least five years ageing in bottle on its lees) it remains youthfully fresh with notes of lemon citrus and honey. With several years additional age, it becomes deliciously toasty. This is serious Champagne to be savoured and enjoyed at your leisure.

>> **Cuvée des Sires La Pelle 2002**

Le Snob ESSENTIAL This sublime wine is only made in the very best vintages and comes from a tiny 0.66 hectare plot near the cemetery in Aÿ. It is part vinified in oak barrels and has a low dosage of just 3 g/l. Ripe, rich and powerfully structured with a noticeable mineral element, this is a deliciously complex wine with a pronounced buttery creaminess and great length.

Vallée de la Marne

René Geoffroy

4, Rue Jeanson, 51160 Aÿ

Tel: +33 (0)3 26 55 32 31
www.champagne-geoffroy.com

Formerly based in the top *premier cru* village of Cumières where the family's 14 hectares of vineyards are located, Jean-Baptiste Geoffroy now has a brand new winery in nearby Aÿ. This passionate winemaker is excited about the quality of juice he gets here from two reconditioned traditional presses, a gravity-fed system that allows minimal handling and the space to keep small parcels of wine separately, which increases his blending options.

» ### Cuvée Empreinte NV

The blend for this wine varies harvest to harvest but it's mainly Pinot Noir, with at least half (sometimes all) vinified in large oak *foudres* to help develop complexity and the evolution of the wine. Mellow, ripe and rich on the nose it retains a nice zippy edge, thanks partly to the low dosage of 6–7 g/l.

» ### Volupté Tête de Cuvée

From some of their oldest vineyards in Cumières, usually a Chardonnay and Pinot Noir blend in 2005. the cuvée was 100 per cent Chardonnay – 50 per cent fermented in large oak *foudres*, the other half in *barriques*. The first sensation is of full and ripe fruit but there is an underlying brisk acidity and a fresh finish.

» ### Millésimé 2000 Extra Brut

Again, Chardonnay is dominant in this extra brut blend, which has just 2 g/l dosage. A bright, light gold in colour, this was a ripe harvest, it's 100 per cent fermented in used Burgundian oak barrels. Reticent at first, this cuvée needs time to open up in the glass, revealing a full and rich palate, a chalky mineral note and an impressively long finish.

Bruno Michel

4, Allée de la Vieille Ferme, 51530 Pierry

Tel: +33 (0)3 26 55 10 54

Grower Bruno Michel is a Pinot Meunier specialist like his father, José Michel, who was famous for his collection of older vintages, though he also has Chardonnay and Pinot Noir planted. He farms some 15 hectares of vineyards, mainly organically. He vinifies his wines partly in oak (the vintage cuvées are wholly fermented in oak) and partly in stainless steel, and also keeps his reserve wines in oak.

» Cuvée Blanche

This entry-level wine is a blend of 50 per cent Chardonnay and 50 per cent Pinot Meunier, based on the 2004 harvest with 30 per cent reserve wine from 2003. It is both mellow and soft, and rounded while really fresh and energetic, a style that makes for very enjoyable drinking.

» Premier Cru Blanc de Blancs NV Brut

An attractive wine combining freshness, richness and complexity, it is made from even amounts of the 2003 and 2004 harvests, which is vinified in oak and stays in wood for 10 months prior to bottling. It is surprisingly fresh given the oak regime but with an attractive richness in the mouth and some spiciness.

» Cuvée Special 2000

Le Snob ESSENTIAL Made 100 per cent from Pinot Meunier, aged one year in oak, this gives off aromas of the forest floor after rain and has a distinctive mushroom truffley note. It is a very vinous expression of champagne that comes from Bruno's best 50-year-old Pinot Meunier vines.

>> **'Les Rosés'**

This single-vineyard *saignée* rosé comes from a specific plot of 45-year-old vines in St Agnan near Dormans. It's of a wine real character and complexity, with exotic aromas of ripe mango, a spicy element and a deliciously creamy texture.

Côte des Blancs

Agrapart & Fils

57, Avenue Jean Jaures, 51190 Avize

Tel: +33 (0)3 26 57 51 38
www.champagne-agrapart.com

Pascal and Fabrice Agrapart own 9.75 hectares of prime vineyard, the majority in the *grands crus* villages of Avize, Oger, Cramant and Oiry divided into 62 separate plots. These plots are all vinified separately in oak, making use of natural yeasts, with minimal intervention. No chemical pesticides or weed killers are used here, the vineyards are ploughed and the wines are never chaptalised.

>> **Les 7 Crus**

A two-vintage blend (in this case 2007 with reserve wine from 2006) of four *grands crus* and three *premiers crus*. The dosage is just 7 g/l. A quarter is aged in large old oak *demi-muids*, the rest in stainless steel. The result is a gentle harmonious non-vintage cuvée with creamy notes and a fine taut minerality.

Words from the wise

Alistair Viner Wine buyer,
Harrods, London

» **Vintage value**

The majority of champagne sales are non-vintage
but then there is a leap to much more expensive
prestige cuvées while the vintage sector tends to get
forgotten. But vintage often offers quality for far less
money. You get a beautiful representation of house
style, slightly different vintage to vintage because it is
all from a single year. The wines are mostly quite
mature when first sold, but will often age further
attractively. At the moment there are some very fine
years available like 2002, plus some '99s that also
impress, such as Gosset and Pol Roger Blanc de
Blancs, which is exceptional wine. Outside of sherry
there isn't another sector of the fine wine market
where older vintages are so readily available.

They are also terrific value; while prestige cuvées
are mainly over £100, there is a selection of top
vintages between £45 and £75, for example, Joseph
Perrier's Blanc de Blancs and vintage rosé, both from
2002, are under £60 a bottle.

Franck Bonville

9, Rue Pasteur, 51190 Avize

Tel: +33 (0)3 26 57 52 30
www.champagne-franck-bonville.com

Established by Franck Bonville in 1937, this family business is now run by his son Gilles and grandson Olivier, who is the winemaker. He has 18 hectares of prime vineyard in the *grands crus* of Cramant, Avize and Oger. His aim is to express the freshness and mineral qualities of this great chalky terroir.

>> **Cuvée Sélection Brut NV**

This is an excitingly fresh, lifted and mineral Blanc de Blancs style, with reserve wine giving it extra depth, length and complexity. It's all made from *grand cru* Chardonnay. The current cuvée is from a harvest base of 2007 (70 per cent) with reserve wine from 2006 (30 per cent), and a dosage of 9.5 g/l.

>> **Les Belles Voyes**

This cuvée is all vinified (and aged for seven months) in oak and produced from the best vineyard parcels in Oger. The oak adds a vinous gloss of richness and an extra layer of complexity, making this a particularly food-friendly wine.

>> **Millesimé 2004 Grand Cru Blanc de Blancs Brut**

Le Snob ESSENTIAL A blend of two grand cru terroirs, Avize and Oger, this lovely champagne is fresh and lifted with a soft cushion of tiny bubbles that give it a beautiful creamy texture in the mouth. There's a quite developed biscuity note, great balance and a polished finish that leaves you wanting more. Top class.

Claude Cazals

28, Rue du Grand Mont,
51190 Le Mesnil-sur-Oger

+33 (0) 3 26 57 52 26
www.champagne-claude-cazals.net

This family business in Le Mesnil-sur-Oger is run by
Delphine Cazals (who is married to Olivier Bonville
of Franck Bonville in Avize) and has 9 hectares of
grands and *premiers crus* vineyards in the Côte des
Blancs. This includes a 3.7-hectare walled *clos* in
Oger, where the oldest vines planted in the 1950s
have been used each year since 1995 to make the
single vineyard Le Clos Cazals.

» Le Clos Cazals 1998

Le Snob ESSENTIAL The grapes in the
beautifully-situated *clos*
regularly attain an extra degree of
maturity thanks to the shelter
afforded by the walls and the aspect
of the vines. The 1998 vintage was a
golden coloured, lusciously rich,
silken textured, honeyed wine of
pure hedonistic drinking
pleasure. Burnished sunshine
in a glass with the richness
and mouthfeel of top
Meursault, plus terrific
length. Only 4,000 bottles
and 200 magnums are made
each year.

Cuvée Vive Grand Cru Extra Brut NV

A lovely light-gold hue, this wine exudes ripe, stoned fruit aromas of quince with a note of honey. While it has good fresh acidity, it's more about generous fruit ripeness belying its low dosage. There is a buttery note and some biscuit mouthfeel, and just a note of minerality on the finish.

Pierre Gimonnet & Fils

1, Rue de la République, 51530 Cuis

Tel: +33 (0)3 26 59 78 70
www.champagne-gimonnet.com

The Blanc de Blancs champagnes made by brothers Didier and Olivier Gimonnet are exemplary Côte des Blancs Chardonnays: taut, intense, mineral-edged wines of finesse and elegance. They make good use of their 26 hectares of vineyard: half are in the *grands crus* villages of Cramant and Chouilly, the rest in the highly regarded *premier cru* of Cuis.

» Gimonnet Cuis Premier Cru Brut NV

This cuvée has a harvest base of 2005 with reserve wines from 2004, 2002 and 1999, themselves assemblages with older component parts, which adds complexity. It has a light dosage of just 8 g/l. Brisk and zesty with a lifted grapefruit zing to it, this champagne is a great, refreshing pick-me-up but also has some chalky minerality. It seems to get more impressive year after year.

» Brut Gastronome 2004

Le Snob ESSENTIAL A blend of Chardonnays from Chouilly (49 per cent), Cuis (39.8 per cent) and Cramant (11.2 per cent), makes this wine brilliantly lively. It also has some spiciness and a lovely developed palate texture and mouth feel. A class act.

Champagne André Jacquart

63, Avenue de Bammental, 51130 Vertus

Tel: + 33 (0)3 26 57 52 29
www.couleursdoyard.com

In 2004, a dynamic new generation took over this grower that boasts a 24-hectare estate. Brother and sister Benoit and Marie Doyard built a completely new winery and now produce just four champagnes using the best fruit from their *premiers* and *grands crus* vineyards in Vertus and Le Mesnil-sur-Oger. They have halved their annual production, down to around 80,000 bottles, in the search for quality. Their new Experience range was launched in

Sweet to dry

As recently as the mid 19th century all champagne was made in a sweet style. These days dosage levels in most commercial champagnes have come down on average. 'Doux' is the sweetest, with a dosage level above 50 g/l but very little is made, while in the 1850s there were many wines with over twice that. The move towards 'brut' styles began in the 1870s but it was over a century before any sizeable house, Laurent-Perrier in this case, launched a zero-dosage champagne in the shape of Ultra Brut, in 1981.

January 2008 – all the wines undergo some oak fermentation, dosage levels have been reduced to a very low 3 g/l and each bears a date of disgorgement.

❯❯ Brut Experience Premier Cru NV

Made from a blend of *premier* and *grand cru* Chardonnay, this wine is part oak-fermented but doesn't undergo malolactic fermentation, which helps to preserve the exhilarating freshness to good effect. It's a concentrated, mineral and lifted Blanc de Blancs style, more accessible in its youth than its counterpart Mesnil *Grand Cru* brut.

❯❯ Mesnil Experience Grand Cru Brut NV

Le Snob ESSENTIAL This impressive fizz is based on the 2004 harvest with around 10 per cent reserve wine. While 80 per cent of it is barrel fermented, such treatment barely tames the Mesnil fruit; the wine remained quite linear and steely on initial release but with recognisable concentration and mineral power. Now, after additional years of ageing, it has blossomed into something richer, more complex and aromatically expressive with toasty, smoky notes and a long evolved finish.

Larmandier-Bernier

19, Avenue du Général de Gaulle, 51130 Vertus

Tel: +33 (0)3 26 52 13 24 www.larmandier.fr

Arguably the most respected and admired grower-producer in the whole of Champagne, Pierre Larmandier remains self-effacingly modest although his wines have achieved critical acclaim worldwide. His vineyards are farmed biodynamically, and he uses oak barrels and large oak *foudres* to ferment much of the base wine and store their reserves. Winemaking and attention to detail are meticulous, and the wines are stunning right across the range.

>> **Tradition Premier Cru Vertus NV**
A blend of 85 per cent Chardonnay and 15 per cent Pinot Noir, this is a little less Pinot Noir than it has been in the past. The harvest base is 2007, with 30 per cent reserve wine stored in casks and oak vats in a kind of solera system (the oldest from the 2002 harvest). With a ripe, full nose and purity of fruit, it has a low dosage at just 4 g/l, but it is still rich and keeps minerality, with a salty note on the tongue.

>> **Terre de Vertus Premier Cru (non-dosé)**
Le Snob ESSENTIAL This wine comes from two parcels of mid-slope vineyard in Vertus, the individual qualities of which Pierre only discovered in blind tastings. Lemon yellow with gold highlights, explosively fresh but rich in the mouth, it has it has ripe developed aromas, with a very noticeable biscuity texture. It is impressively powerful and complex with a very long finish.

>> **Blanc de Blancs Premier Cru Vertus NV Extra Brut**
This has a different nose – not the roundness and richness of the blend but ripe fruit and an early spicy note. There is good freshness but the emphasis is more on the minerality. It has a quite developed creamy palate feel and

biscuity mouth texture, some honeyed notes and a long finish. With more time it will develop further complexity. Made from a 2007 harvest base, the Vertus Chardonnay component comes from the chalkier northern part of the *cru* and is blended with *grand cru* Chardonnay from Cramant and Oger and a large portion of reserve wine.

» Rosé de Saignée Premier Cru (Vertus)

Presented in a frosted bottle, this is made entirely from the 2007 harvest and so could be vintage. A light ruby-red colour, achieved by two to three days maceration, it has aromas of red fruits and is made in a very clean and fresh style. The initial red fruits evolve into black fruits in the mouth.

» Vielles Vignes de Cramant Grand Cru 2005

Less obvious or open on the nose initially, nonetheless, this wine has a very developed rich palate and a luxuriant creamy texture with distinctive biscuity notes. It has almost no dosage at just 2 g/l, but you wouldn't know that, as this is a complex wine of real intensity and richness that changes constantly in the glass, gradually revealing more complexity.

» Cooperatives

Developing investments

Less than a quarter of the cooperatives operating in Champagne actually sell the finished product and between them they account for just 10 per cent of worldwide champagne sales. However, aware of the need to be competitive, and in an effort to sell more wines at a higher price level to boost the income of their grape growers, the top co-ops have invested heavily in the latest equipment over the past couple of decades and some now make serious-quality champagne. Several have always had good access to the best grapes through the *grands crus* and *premiers crus* vineyards owned by their grower members and now they have the technical know-how and winemaking kit to take full advantage of this.

Reims

De Castelnau

5, Rue Gosset, 51066 Reims

Tel: +33 (0)3 26 77 89 00
www.champagne-de-castelnau.eu

The De Castelnau brand is produced by the Cooperative Regionale des Vins de Champagne of Reims (CRVC), which has some 640-grower members who own 825 hectares of vineyard, more than half in *premiers* and *grands crus*. As well as being able to source grapes from these top vineyards the CRVC boasts one of the best respected winemakers in Champagne, Richard Dailly, who has been working with this co-op for nearly 20 years and is a highly skilled blender.

» De Castelnau Brut NV
Thanks to extra ageing (typically four years before release) and the extensive use of reserve wines adding depth and complexity, this cuvée has an attractively, soft-textured and quite developed rich style.

» De Castelnau Cuvée Spéciale Millésimé 2002
This is the first vintage of this cuvée, which has a higher proportion of Chardonnay (61 per cent) in the blend than the regular vintage offering, and it benefits from the high quality of '02 Chardonnay, which gives the wine an attractive buttery richness with aromas of white peach and a honeyed note, plus good length.

» De Castelnau Brut Rosé NV
Le Snob ESSENTIAL This wine is decently fruity and made in a soft creamy style. It is one of the most enjoyably drinkable non-vintage pink fizzes on the market and great value for money.

Jacquart

34, Boulevard Lundy, 51100 Reims

Tel: +33 (0)3 26 07 88 40
www.champagne-jacquart.fr

The Jacquart brand is produced by Alliance Champagne which is co-owned by three different coooperative groups that are spread across the region; one in Château Thierry to the western edge of the appellation nearest Paris, another is located fairly centrally in Aÿ, while the third is in the southernmost Côte des Bar vineyard near to Troyes. With its members owning 2,300 hectares of vineyard spread across the appellation, this gives Alliance lots of blending options for the production of the Jacquart range.

» Jacquart Brut de Nominée NV

Le Snob ESSENTIAL This is the cognoscenti's pick of the range, a roughly 50/50 Chardonnay and Pinot Noir blend with a lovely balance and bright citrus highlights. It develops a sumptuous richness over time but retains good refreshing acidity too.

» Jacquart Brut Grand Millésime 2000

This opulent, toasty and nicely mature blend of 55 per cent Pinot Noir, 45 per cent Chardonnay is only available now under the Jacquart Oenothèque range, but it is worth seeking out, especially in magnum where the freshness is accentuated.

Montagne de Reims

Mailly Grand Cru

28, Rue de la Libération, 51500 Mailly

Tel: +33 (0)3 26 49 41 10 www.champagne-mailly.com

The Grand Cru cooperative at Mailly in the Montagne de Reims is a good example of how the best cooperatives have invested significantly in upgrading their wineries over the past decade or so. Owned by 77 growers from 25 families, this co-op boasts 70 hectares of prime *grand cru* vineyard all around the village of Mailly, three-quarters of it planted with Pinot Noir, the rest with Chardonnay. It produces mainly rich, full-bodied Pinot Noir-led wines, of great intensity and vigour, that need time to mellow and show at their best.

» Extra Brut

This cuvée, a three-way blend of 2005, 2004 and 2003 harvests, has no dosage and really needs the additional ageing time it gets before release. Even after five years maturing it is still very lively and fresh, with a noticeable mineral note and a long fine linear finish.

» Les Enchansons Millésime 1999

Le Snob ESSENTIAL At the top of the impressive Mailly range this glorious concentrated Pinot Noir-dominated blend has a rich golden colour and seductive richness but also a long life ahead if you cellar it further. Like most of their range it's three parts Pinot Noir to one part Chardonnay and

» The influence of oak

Most champagne houses used to ferment their wines in oak barrels but outside traditional producers like Alfred Gratien, Bollinger and Krug, its use declined in the 1950s and 1960s. Stainless steel became the norm, however, there is a trend among smaller quality houses and a new generation of growers to return to oak, particularly for the initial fermentation (some also part age their wines in oak before bottling).

Fermentation in oak doesn't necessarily result in overtly oaky champagnes as most producers use old barrels that don't impart woody flavours to the wines and many use large *foudres* of 2,000 litres or more capacity where the ratio of wood to wine is very low.

The attraction of oak is the contact with the air, or what is known as micro-oxygenation. If the wine has the structure and personality to handle it, this process helps bring out aromas and flavour, adding complexity. It also has a beneficial effect of making the wine less prone to oxidation.

comes from some of their best and oldest vineyard parcels. It is a wine of considerable complexity.

» Exception Blanche Millésime 1999

A real rarity, this is a special vintage Blanc de Blancs style that combines Mailly Chardonnay with that from another cooperative (Les Viticulteurs d'Avize) based in Avize. The richness and fullness of Mailly Chardonnay combines with the power and intensity of Avize to produce a penetrating and vivid wine that has a floral and citrus element and at this stage only a suggestion of the complexity that maturity will bring. It needs lavish food like crayfish or lobster to show at its best.

Coteaux Champenois

A very small volume of still wine is produced in Champagne under the Coteaux Champenois appellation, most of it red. It is hard to buy outside the region and typically produced by small growers based in *crus* like Bouzy, Aÿ, Ambonnay and Cumières where mostly black grapes are planted. At their best in warm years, where black grapes get notably ripe, the wines tend to be like very light fruity burgundies, though critics say they are nearly always thin and acidic, which demonstrates why Champagne became a region specialising in sparkling wine not table wine.

Vallée de la Marne

Beaumont des Crayères

64, Rue de la Liberté, 51530 Mardeuil

Tel: +33 (0)3 26 55 29 40
www.champagne-beaumont.com

The Beaumont des Crayères brand is produced by a medium-sized co-op located in the village of Mardeuil on the north side of the Vallée de la Marne, where most of the 200-odd growers are part-timers who tend the vines (on over 86 hectares) at the weekends or on holidays. It's a characterful range that hits a highpoint with 'Nostalgie' vintage, a classy act at a very good price.

» **Grande Réserve Brut NV**

A high percentage of Pinot Meunier in this blend accentuates the red berry fruit flavours and helps make it an enjoyably forward, supplely mellow wine with a nutty note on the finish.

» **Fleur Noir 2003 Brut Vintage**

A Blancs de Noirs made from the super-ripe precocious 2003 harvest that's a blend of 70 per cent Pinot Noir and 30 per cent Pinot Meunier. Exuberantly fruity with some very attractive red berry juiciness and refreshing acidity it's creamy textured and seductive. A real charmer.

» **Nostalgie Brut Vintage 1999**

Le Snob ESSENTIAL The co-op's top of the range cuvée is a 65/35 Chardonnay-Pinot Noir blend of impressive length and quality. Described by the cognoscenti as a 'mini-Krug', with quince-like fruit and a buttery, savoury, toasty palate many could be fooled. In the glass it just gets better and better as it opens up.

Pannier

23, Rue Roger-Catillon, 02407 Château-Thierry
Tel: +33 (0)3 23 69 51 30
www.champagnepannier.com

Champagne Pannier was founded by Louis Eugene Pannier in 1899, in the village Dizy, adjacent to Epernay. In 1937, his son purchased medieval cellars in Château-Thierry, in the Marne Valley and transferred his thriving champagne business there. The brand and the business were bought by a group of wine growers (COVAMA) in 1974 and this co-op now processes enough grapes to vinify over 4 million bottles. COVAMA, which is part of Alliance Champagne, is also involved in the production of the Jacquart brand.

» Égérie de Pannier Rosé de Saignée Brut NV

Le Snob ESSENTIAL A very pretty pale pink it has a lovely, perfumed floral nose with hints of fresh raspberries, while in the mouth it's delicate, poised and beautifully balanced with a creamy mouthfeel. A hugely enjoyable and classy pink fizz, delicate yet intense.

» Égérie de Pannier Extra Brut Vintage 2000

The rich golden colour suggests a ripeness that is delivered, with stone fruit aromas and a full, soft luscious texture plus some savoury, mocha notes.

Words from the wise

Mark Jenner Bar Manager,
Coburg Bar, London

» A champagne experience

Champagne evokes a perfect balance between mystery and wonder that has bewitched successive generations. It should be treated with a lightness of touch and a reverence saved for the oldest and rarest of liquids.

Glassware is paramount, I opt for two styles of Riedel glass, the Cuvée Prestige for most non-vintage or, for something that has a little more age to it, the Sauvignon Blanc to really bring out its full potential of expressions, to release the plethora of different aromas.

Sourcing and storage are key, especially in rare vintage cases. Provenance must be traceable right back to the Maison itself, as many top wines are traded like commodities and could have travelled the globe. Dedicated EuroCave wine storage systems are the best type of storage, set at a consistent temperature between 7–8°C, mirroring the caves in which these wines were born.

Côte des Blancs

Nicolas Feuillatte CVC

Chouilly, 51206 Epernay

Tel: +33 (0)3 26 59 55 50 www.feuillatte.com

The Feuillatte brand is produced by the largest cooperative group in Champagne, based in Chouilly. Its 4,900 members between them own nearly one-fifth (over 6,000 hectares) of the appellation's vineyards, which gives winemaker Jean-Pierre Vincent a huge palate of blending options to experiment with. With access to 13 of Champagne's 17 *grand cru* vineyards he has made some very fine single *cru* wines and this range has now evolved into Grand Cru Pinot Noir and Grand Cru Chardonnay. There are also two oak-aged styles under the Cuvée 225 label. While the main non-vintage brand has become one of the top five selling champagnes worldwide, the most exciting wines are these niche products often produced in relatively small quantities.

» **Cuvée Palmes d'Or 1999**

Le Snob ESSENTIAL This vintage is quite a contrast to the lusher, full-bodied '98 wine that preceded it, with more elegance and a noticeable chalky minerality on the palate. It's a 50/50 Pinot Noir-Chardonnay blend; the latter is a combination of fine citrus Chardonnays from the *Grands Crus* Côtes de Blancs villages of Chouilly, Cramant and Le Mesnil-sur-Oger contrasted with the rich, ripe tropical fruit notes of Chardonnay from Montgueux that adds a perceptible power and fatness.

» Cuvée 225 Vintage Rosé 2004

A blend of equal proportions of Chardonnay and Pinot Noir with between 15 and 20 per cent of red wine added for the colour, to create a fine coppery pink. This strawberry-fruited rosé is a new addition to the range to complement the white Cuvée 225, and like that wine it is all barrel-fermented in oak. But while this is a quite weighty, distinctive, savoury style with some vanilla notes it is not overtly oaky, nor heavy, as the component *crus* in the blend can handle this treatment.

Le Mesnil Cooperative

58, Grande-Rue, 51190 Mesnil-sur-Oger

Tel:+33 (0)3 26 57 53 23
www.champagnelemesnil.com

Based in the heart of the *grand cru* village of Le Mesnil-sur-Oger, this cooperative has around 500 members who between them own some 305 hectares of vineyards. The co-op mainly supplies the major *négociant* houses with top-quality still wines (*vins clairs*) for their brands. But it makes some wine and its top cuvée Sublime lives up to its name and, as the re-released 1988 vintage shows, can age fantastically well.

>> **Le Mesnil Brut Vintage 2004**

This still-youthful, all-Chardonnay fizz from the forward 2004 vintage is a slightly more generous, fuller style than some Blancs de Blancs champagnes though it doesn't lack edge or concentration and will develop increasingly greater complexity over time.

Union Champagne

7, Rue Pasteur, 51190 Avize

Tel: +33 (0)3 26 57 94 22 www.union-champagne.fr

The 1,800 members of this cooperative between them have the largest group holdings of *grand* (800 hectares) and *premier crus* (400 hectares) in the Côte des Blancs. Much of the produce is sold onto the large houses for use in their top cuvées, but under its own De Saint Gall label, this co-op makes a consistently good range of Blanc de Blancs champagnes.

>> **Cuvée Orpale Blanc de Blancs 1998**

Le Snob ESSENTIAL Their top wine is a fine blend of arguably the four best *grands crus* villages in the Côte des Blancs: Avize, Cramant, Oger and Le Mesnil-sur-Oger. Pure, mineral with a distinctive and penetrating citrusy note, this is a long-keeper of considerable class and a fine example of the style.

» Possess

Buying retail

If you're looking to buy a specific bottle, or are interested in buying to lay down for a few years, it's best to consult the seller or an expert first to find out which ones are likely to develop further, and when you might expect it to reach its peak. You may have to search a little bit harder for specific and vintage champagnes, but there are good retailers around the world and most will have websites as well.

EUROPE

C Comme Champagne,
8, Rue Gambetta, 51200 Epernay, France
Tel: +33 (0)3 26 32 09 55 www.c-comme.fr

La Cave des Filles
463, Avenue du Général Leclerc, 51530 Dizy, France
Tel : +33 (0) 32 26 54 78 38 www.lacavedesfilles.com

La Vinocave
43, Place Drouet d'Erlon, 51100 Reims, France
Tel: +33 (0)3 26 40 60 07

La Cave d'Erlon
40, Place Drouet d'Erlon, 51100 Reims, France
Tel: +33 (0)3 26 47 44 44

Les Caves du Forum
10, rue Courmaux, 51100 Reims, France
Tel: +33 (0)3 26 79 15 15 www.lescavesduforum.com/

Cellier St Pierre
1, Place Saint Pierre, 10000 Troyes, France
Tel: +(0)3 25 80 59 25 www.celliersaintpierre.fr

Alsterhaus, Hamburg
Jungfernstieg 16-20, 20354 Hamburg, Germany
Phone: +49 40 359010 www.alsterhaus.de

Feinkost Dallmayr, München
Dienerstr. 14-15, D-80331 München, Germany
Phone: +49 89 21350 www.dallmayr.de/

Entrepot du Vin, Berlin
Fasanenstr. 42, D-10719 Berlin, Germany
Tel. +49 (0)30 88551727 www.entrepot-du-vin.de/

Harrods
87–135 Brompton Road, Knightsbridge, London SW1X
7XL, UK Tel: +44 (0)207 730 1234 www.harrods.co.uk

Fortnum & Mason
181 Piccadilly, London W1A 1ER, UK
Tel: +44 (0)207 734 8040 www.fortnumandmason.com

Selfridges
400 Oxford Street, London W1A 1AB, UK
Tel: +44 (0)113 369 8040 www.selfridges.com

Berry Bros. & Rudd Limited
3 St. James's Street, London SW1A 1EG, UK
Tel: +44 (0)800 280 2440 www.bbr.com

Jeroboams, Belgravia,
50–52 Elizabeth Street, London SW1W 9PB, UK
Tel: +44 (0) 207 730 8108 www.Jeroboams.co.uk

UNITED STATES

Crush Wine
153 East 57th Street, New York, NY 10022 USA
Tel: +1 212 980 9463 www.crushwineco.com

Astor Wines
399 Lafayette St, New York, NY 10003 USA
Tel:+1 212 674 7500 www.astorwines.com

K&L Wines
3005 El Camino Real, Redwood City, CA 94061 USA
Tel:+1 650 364 8544 www.klwines.com

WEBSITES
www.champagnewines.com
www.farrvintners.com
www.thewinesociety.com
www.justchampagne.co.uk

Rare and collectible items

There isn't much of a market for rare, old vintages of champagne, certainly not one as developed as that for the top wines from Bordeaux. If you are buying as an investment, you should go for complete cases of the most sought-after champagnes from the top vintages. Magnums are more collectible than bottles and tend to fetch proportionately higher prices.

Champagne investments

Three prestige brands dominate the vintage market at the top end: Louis Roederer Cristal, which regularly commands the highest prices; vintage Krug in second place (although '82 Krug tends to sell for more than '82 Cristal); and Dom Pérignon, which is partly less valuable because it is produced in far greater volume.

The picture is complicated by the fact that all three brands have small volumes of library releases that are given extra ageing and are periodically put on sale by the owners of the brands – Dom Pérignon for example usually has two of its Œnoteque releases in the market at any given time.

The rosé versions of Cristal and Dom Pérignon also fetch considerable premiums on their white equivalents. Krug has two single-vineyard wines in Clos du Mesnil and Clos d'Ambonnay, the latter being one of the most collectible champagnes of recent times, especially its initial 1995 vintage

Prices for other top houses prestige cuvées can also be high, especially for mature vintages. Veuve

Clicquot's La Grande Dame, Taittinger's Comte de Champagne, Dom Ruinart, and Pol Roger's Sir Winston Churchill Cuvée also have a following. The 1990 Pol recently fetched more than La Grande Dame and Dom Perignon at auction.

Personal consumption

If you are looking to buy top vintage champagne to lay down for your own future consumption, far better value is to be found with the straight vintage wines of the top houses, and the prices of older champagnes are certainly not astronomic compared with top older vintages from Bordeaux and Burgundy.

The top vintages to go for over the past three decades are 2002, which quite a few top houses are still to release, 1996, 1995, 1990, 1989, 1988, and 1985. There are also some very good 1998 and 1999 releases, top class 1982s and 1983s if you can find them, and Krug 1981 is seen by the Krug family as one of their best vintages of the twentieth century. In the seventies '79 and '75 stand out, while there were five greats in the sixties: '69, '66, '64, '62 and '61 with the latter being the star, like in Bordeaux.

Where to buy

Buying at auction is one of the best options for finding rare bottles, though this market tends to be restricted to the prestige cuvées, apart from on a number of purely online auction sites. Two of the best, with offices and auctions around the world are Sotheby's (www.sothebys.com) and Christie's (www.christies.com). Otherwise, high-end wine merchants sometimes have a good range of older champagnes.

Champagne storage

To store champagne you need a dark, cool place, free of smells and vibration where the temperature fluctuates very little. Humidity is also important: if it is too dry, the corks tend to dry out and cease being an effective seal. The ideal temperature is probably between 10 and 15°C, perhaps towards the lower end of this scale for champagne as the cellar temperatures in the caves of Reims and Epernay are generally somewhere between 11 and 12°C. The deep cellars at Pol Roger are slightly colder than most in Champagne, at around 9.5°C, and some see this as a significant fact in making particularly long-lived wines. Certainly the lower the temperature (within the 10 to 15°C parameter) the more slowly the champagne will evolve, and while no real harm will come to champagne stored at slightly above 15°C, so long as there are not significant fluctuations in temperature, it will develop more rapidly.

If you don't have suitable cellar space in your home you can purchase a special, humidity-controlled wine fridge, though even the largest of these can only store a few dozen bottles. The alternative is to pay for professional storage at a reputable wine merchant that offers this service, which is likely to cost a few pounds per case per year. This could be a good solution if you have large amounts of young wine but it does restrict your ability to open a bottle at will.

Serving and etiquette

One of the leading competitions for sommeliers requires participants to pour equal amounts of champagne from a magnum into 12 glasses, without going back to top any up, avoiding spillage and without pausing while filling a glass, even if it looks like it will overflow. For mere mortals, who may struggle to get the cork out at all, here are some simple guidelines to follow.

Finding the right temperature

To serve, you need a lower temperature than for storage, ideally between 6 and 10°C (towards the higher end for the best mature wines) as this should allow the slow release of the mousse. Too warm and the bottle may be dangerous to open and, once it is, the fizz will be quickly lost. The most efficient way to chill a bottle is in an ice bucket filled with water, plus a big handful of ice cubes, for between 10 and 15 minutes. A couple of hours in the door of a fridge should also be about right, but if you leave it longer than a day, the cork tends to stick, making opening the bottle more difficult.

Opening a bottle

Remove the wire cage that holds the cork in place, being careful to keep your hand over the cork as you do so, to stop it flying out. Then, hold the bottle at a 45-degree angle (take care not to point it at anyone), grip the cork firmly in one hand and, holding the base of the bottle in the other, gradually turn the bottle, not the cork. Once you feel the cork starting to move, hold it down so it comes out slowly 'with a whisper' not a loud pop. Make sure you have a couple of glasses in front of you, just in case the cork does come out rather faster that you intended. Champagne is too expensive to spill on the floor.

Pouring champagne

It is better to put a little wine in each glass first and then go back and top each one up. You can normally fill six or seven appropriate glasses from a single bottle, leaving room in the glass for it to breathe. Use clean glasses – detergent is the enemy of bubbles. The secret is to rinse glasses a couple of times in hot water after washing.

Glassware

Flutes are better than the open flat coupe to preserve the bubbles and capture the wine's aroma – the broad surface of the coupe glass means the bubbles will disappear more quickly. Flutes that are more in the tulip shape are the best, certainly from a tasting point of view. For older vintage champagnes and prestige cuvées, a fine white wine glass is a good alternative.

130

Champagne and food

It's not an accident that most champagne in restaurants is consumed as an aperitif; it's a great appetite stimulator. But it also works very well with a surprisingly large range of foods.

Combine lighter styles with canapés and cocktail nibbles, cashew nuts, or perhaps a brunch of smoked salmon and scrambled eggs. Fresh and lightly cooked seafood (oysters and scallops for example) can be paired with young fresh Blanc de Blancs. In restaurants in Paris and Reims the minerality of some Extra Brut and *non-dosé* cuvées is often matched with shellfish to good effect, sushi and sashimi dishes too.

Champagne also has a natural affinity with luxury ingredients like caviar, lobster and *foie gras*. It's a good foil for the saltiness of caviar, although lobster probably needs a richer aged style of Blanc de Blancs, and for *foie gras*, a good-quality sweeter style or mature old vintage champagne.

For meaty dishes, such as pigeon or other game birds, roast duck, or even rare lamb cutlets, aged vintage rosé majoring on Pinot Noir can be delicious. The toasty richness of great mature champagne from a vintage like a 1988 is mind-blowing with roast turbot or Bresse chicken stuffed with truffles. And finally if you want to end a meal with fine champagne, it goes well with all sorts of cheese but particularly with hard varieties, the likes of Beaufort, Parmesan or extra-aged Cantal.

Champagne cocktails

While some people may argue against mixing champagne, there's no doubt that a champagne cocktail can be an impressive creation. The Classic champagne cocktail is an old favourite, the others are particularly fine modern creations. All of these should be served in a champagne flute.

Classic Champagne Cocktail

25 ml cognac

Brown sugar cube

3 to 4 drops of angostura bitters

100 ml champagne

Carefully drip the angostura bitters onto the sugar cube. Pour the cognac into a flute, add the soaked sugar cube and top up with champagne.

Blushing Bubbles

10 ml passion fruit purée

15 ml raspberry purée

100 ml champagne

Mix together the chilled purées and pour into flute. Top up with champagne slowly and carefully (as it tends to fizz up and overflow). Mix with a long handled spoon.

» Matching champagne with food

When matching food with champagne, *non-dosé* and extra brut styles work well with lighter dishes, while with a butter-based sauce, a higher dosage style is preferable. For a seafood dish, match the wine to the richness of the sauce. Try contrasting a wild mushroom risotto with a Blanc de Noir, ideally a mature vintage style. Less fizziness with greater age means more mouth texture to the champagne, making it ideal for this sort of earthy, creamy dish.

For non-vintage, consider the blend first: a Chardonnay-led style needs freshness and acidity in the dish, whereas Pinot-dominant cuvées work well with more spicy and earthy ingredients. With vintage champagne, contrast the power of the dish with the blend and style of the specific year. I'd choose very different food drinking a 1996, with its marked acidity, than I would to match the ripeness of 1989. Made mostly in a crisp, light and (sometimes) fruity style, non-vintage rosé makes the ideal aperitif.

French 75

15 ml Greenall's Bloom premium gin
5 ml freshly squeezed lemon juice
5 ml gomme syrup
100 ml champagne

Combine the gin, lemon and syrup and shake well. Pour into a flute and top up with champagne.

Luxury Mojito

50 ml Havana 3-year-old rum
4–5 slices of fresh lime
Handful of fresh mint leaves
Brown sugar
40 ml champagne

Muddle the lime, mint and sugar in a pestle and mortar until well mixed then add the rum. Add crushed ice, strain into a flute and top up with champagne.

Champolitain

50 ml Ketel One vodka
50 ml cranberry juice
25 ml Cointreau
freshly squeezed lime
Champagne to top up with

Pour the vodka, juices and Cointreau into a cocktail shaker filled with ice. Shake and strain into a chilled cocktail glass. Top up with a little champagne.

» Discover

Champagne bars

There are many bars and restaurants around the world that stock a good range of champagnes. To help you find particularly impressive examples, below is a selection of those that are really worth hunting out whether it is for their range, rare vintages, great value or, in the best, a combination of all three.

EUROPE

Le Bar 228 Le Meurice, 228, Rue de Rivoli, 75001 Paris
Tel: +33 (0)144 58 10 10 www.lemeurice.com

Le Bar du Plaza Athénée 25, Avenue Montaigne, 75008 Paris
Tel: +33 (0)1 53 67 66 60 www.bar-plaza-athenee-paris.com

Flûte l'Etoile 19 Rue de l'Etoile, 75017 Paris
Tel: +33 (0)1 45 72 10 14 www.flutebar.com

Bar München Maximilianstrasse 36, 80539 Munich
Tel: +49 89 22 90 90 www.barmuenchen.com

Schumann's Bar Odeonsplatz 6&7, 80539 Munich
Tel: +49 89 22 90 60 www.schumanns.de

Feinkost Käfer Prinzregentenstrasse 73, 81675 Munich
Tel:+49 89 41 680 Munich www.feinkost-kaefer.de

Hotel Louis C Jacob Elbchaussee 401–403, 22609 Hamburg
Tel: +49 40 82 25 50 www.hotel-jacob.de

Grill Royal Friedrichstrasse 105b, 10117 Berlin
Tel: +49 30 28 87 92 88 www.grillroyal.com

Ritz Carlton Potsdamer Platz 3, 10785 Berlin
Tel: +49 30 33 77 77 www.ritzcarlton.com

Hammers Weinkostbar Körtestraße 20, 10967 Berlin-Kreuzberg Tel: +49 30 69 81 86 77 www.hammers-wein.de

Rutz Weinbar Chausseestraße 8, 10115 Berlin
Tel: +49 30 24 62 87 60 www.rutz-weinbar.de

Bubbles Champagne Bar Sadovaya Triumfalnaya Street, 10/13, Building 1, Moscow Tel: +7 495 694 6987

Kalina Bar Novinsky Boulevard, No 8, Building Lotte Plaza, 21st floor, Moscow Tel: +7 495 229 5519 www.kalinabar.ru

Texture Restaurant & Champagne Bar 34 Portman Street, London W1H 7BY Tel: +44 (0)207 224 0028 www.texture-restaurant.co.uk

St Pancras Champagne Bar St Pancras Station, Pancras Road, Camden Town, London NW1 2QP Tel: +44 (0)207 843 7688 www.searcys.co.uk

The Coburg Bar The Connaught Hotel, Carlos Place, Mayfair, London W1K 2AL Tel: +44 (0)207 499 7070 www.the-connaught.co.uk

Amuse Bouche 51 Parsons Green Lane, Fulham, London SW6 4JA Tel: +44 (0)207 371 8517 www.abcb.co.uk

Epernay Wine Bar The Electric Press Building, 12 Great George Street, Leeds LS1 3DW Tel: +44 (0)113 242 9977 www.epernaychampagnebars.com

The Harrow at Little Bedwyn Marlborough, Wiltshire SN8 3JP Tel: +44 (0)1672 870 871 www.theharrowatlittlebedwyn.co.uk

The Bell at Skenfrith Monmouthshire NP7 8UH Tel: +44 (0)1600 750 235 www.skenfrith.co.uk

UNITED STATES

The Bubble Lounge San Francisco 714 Montgomery Street, San Francisco, CA 94111 Tel: +1 415 434 4204

The Bubble Lounge New York 228 West Broadway, New York, NY 10013 Tel: +1 212 431 3433 www.bubblelounge.com

Champagne Bar The Plaza New York, 768 Fifth Avenue, New York, NY 10019 Tel: +1 212 759 3000 www.theplaza.com/dining/champagne-bar/

Del Posto 85 Tenth Avenue, New York, NY 10011 Tel: +1 212 497 8090 www.delposto.com

Terroir 413 East Twelfth Street, New York, NY 10009 Tel: +1 646 602 1300 www.wineisterroir.com

Pops for Champagne 601 North State Street, Chicago, IL 60611, Tel: +1 312 266 7677 www.popsforchampagne.com

Laguna Champagne Bar The Palazzo, 3325 Las Vegas Blvd South, Las Vegas, NV 89109 Tel:+1 702 607 7777 www.palazzo.com

Champagne travel

To find champagne worthy of the name and experience all the region has to offer, you have to go there. Only in Champagne can you source stock at the major houses, brought up from their own deep, cool chalk cellars where all the wine matures in perfect conditions.

The three main centres of Reims, Epernay and Troyes have plenty to offer the wine-loving visitor. In Reims and Epernay there are impressive tours of some of the major houses spectacular cellars. All three towns offer visitors the chance to buy unusual cuvées, growers' champagnes and older vintages not usually seen outside France, plus plenty of high-quality restaurants.

Cellar tours

While in the region you'll probably want to visit a cellar or two. The Romans originally dug out these *crayères* in their search for building materials, carving out great blocks of chalk that amazingly were hauled out of the narrow necks to the pits by ropes. The oldest cellars still run in line to the southern side of Reims, grouped around the Place du Général Gouraud, and this is where you will find the houses of Pommery, Taittinger, Veuve Clicquot and Ruinart. The other side of the city GH Mumm has a cellar tour that's well worth trying.

The most spectacular cellars to visit are arguably at Pommery, where once you have climbed down the 116 steps, you can clearly see the huge conical shaped chalk pits that were excavated by the Romans. As a bonus here there are also dramatic giant carvings, made by Gustave Navlet in the 1880s, which are literally hewn out of the soft, chalky walls of the *crayères*. Ruinart also has an impressive cellar in Reims, with steps descending 30 metres into the vast subterranean cathedral-like chalk *crayères*.

GH Mumm
29, Rue du Champ de Mars, 51053 Reims
Tel: +33 (0)3 26 49 59 69 www.mumm.com

Pommery
5, Place du Général Gouraud, 51689 Reims
Tel: +33 (0)3 26 61 62 63 www.pommery.com

Ruinart
4, Rue des Crayères, 51100 Reims
Tel: +33 (0)3 26 77 51 51 www.ruinart.com

Taittinger
9, Place Saint-Nicaise, 51100 Reims
Tel: +33 (0)3 26 85 43 35 www.taittinger.com

Vineyards

While visiting the major houses dotted around the city you'll find some wines that are not exported. To buy growers' champagnes, which if you find the right addresses offer some of the top wines and best deals in Champagne, you really have to leave the confines of the city and head out into the vineyard. You could easily visit several in a leisurely morning or afternoon tour, though ideally you should contact them in advance to check availability. Here you are buying wine directly from the people who make it. There is no better way of learning about champagne.

For something out of the ordinary some growers organise special *Jour de vendange* trips during the harvest, typically in mid-September, when you have the chance to pick and press grapes and also try the champagnes made by some small producers. Complete lists of wine growers, offering these grape-harvest days, are available from the Aube (Tel: +33 (0)3 25 42 50 00) and Marne Tourist Boards (Tel: +33 (0)3 26 68 37 52).

Further contacts

For more information on visiting the region the following contacts are useful. The Le Comité interprofessional du vin de Champagne (CIVC), listed below, also has 13 offices outside France in champagne's main markets around the world.

CIVC
Epernay at 5, Rue Henri Martin, 51200 Epernay
Tel: +33 (0)3 26 51 19 30 www.champagne.fr

Reims tourist office
2, Rue Guillaume de Machault, 51100 Reims
Tel: +33 (0)8 92 70 13 51 www.reims-tourisme.com

Epernay tourist office
7, Avenue de Champagne, 512011 Epernay
Tel: +33 (0)3 26 53 33 00 www.ot-epernay.fr

Troyes tourist office
16, Boulevard Carnot, 10000 Troyes
Tel: +33 (0)3 25 82 62 70
www.tourisme-troyes.com

Syndicat Général des Vignerons
Les Champagnes de Vignerons, 17–19 Avenue de Champagne, 51205 Epernay, Tel: +33 (0)3 26 59 55 00
www.champagnesdevignerons.com

Glossary

Assemblage Putting together a blend of different wines and/or years.

Autolysis A bi-chemical process during which yeast cells are broken down.

Barrique A small oak barrel of 225 or 228 litres, as typically used in Bordeaux and Burgundy respectively.

Bottle-age The amount of time a wine spends in bottle before it is consumed, such ageing has a mellowing effect.

Chef de Cave Literally, the cellarmaster who is typically the winemaker, or chief blender.

Cooperative-manipulante (CM) A co-operative making and selling champagne.

Crémant A gently sparkling wine with around 3.5 atmospheres of pressure. Since 1994 the name is no longer allowed in Champagne, although a few producers still make such wines. It is kept for sparkling wines from other parts of France.

Cru Literally, 'growth', as in *premier cru* (first growth). It refers to a specific commune or village.

Cuvée The juice from the first and best pressing of the grapes. It also refers to a specific champagne blend.

Crayère A Gallo-Roman chalk pit dug out for building materials, now used as cellars.

Dégorgement Disgorging – the removal of the deposit that forms in a champagne bottle after the secondary fermentation is complete.

Demi-muid A large wooden barrel, mostly made of oak, of around 600 litres capacity.

Échelle des crus Literally, 'ladder of growths', this is a percentile rating scale by which all 319 *crus* are assessed.

Foudre A large wooden cask.

Grand(s) cru(s) The best vineyards, all rated 100% on the *Échelle des crus*.

Gyropalette A computerised riddling (*remuage*) system in a metal cube-shaped container, typically holding 500 bottles.

Lees A sediment typically made from dead yeast cells which fall to the bottom of the barrel or tank in the winemaking process.

Liqueur de dosage The sugar levels added to a bottle of champagne when it is disgorged (expressed in grams of sugar per litre). It is typically made from mature wine and sugar.

Liqueur de tirage A liqueur added to the still wine to create the secondary fermentation in the bottle.

Marc term for a single pressing of grapes 4,000kgs, amount that is processed in a traditional basket press.

Méthode traditionelle The classic way of making sparkling wine where the secondary fermentation that creates the bubbles takes place in the bottle as opposed to the tank method, in which carbon dioxide is added to the wine.

Monocru Champagne from a single *cru* or village.

Mousse The stream of bubbles in a glass of sparkling wine.

Mousseux Fully sparkling wine with 5 to 6 atmospheres of pressure.

Négociant-manipulant (NM) Champagne merchant who may buy grapes or wines from others to blend their wines.

NV Non-vintage.

Pièce a small oak barrel, usually 205 litres in Champagne.

Premier(s) cru(s) a village or commune rated 90–99 per cent on the *Échelle des crus*.

Prise de mousse the creation of the mousse by the secondary fermentation in bottle.

Pupitres Wooden containers with holes in them into which the bottles of champagne fit for the *remuage* process.

Récoltant-manipulant (RM) A grower making champagne from their own grapes, although they are permitted to buy or swap with another grower up to 5 per cent of their harvest.

Remuage (riddling) The process of turning, twisting, shaking and gradually tilting bottles to encourage the sediment deposit to gradually settle in the neck of the bottle on the crown cap or cork.

Saignée A method of making rosé, in which pigment is bled from the grape skins.

Reserve wines Older wines from previous harvests kept back for blending purposes.

Taille The juice from the second or third pressing of grapes and thus inferior.

Vendage Harvest.

Vigneron A wine grower.

Vins clairs The term used for still wines that have gone through their first but not secondary fermentation.

Index

143

144